MW00451122

NO MATTER WHAT

You've Got to Live Your Dreams.

RON MITCHELL

With JEREMIE GUY

NO MATTER WHAT

You've got to live your dreams.

©Copyright by Ronald Mitchell 2014

All Rights Reserved

No part of this book may be reproduced in any form, by photocopying or by any electronic or mechanical means, including information storage or retrieval systems, without permission in writing from both the copyright owner and the publisher of this book.

Edited by Russell D. James, James Literary Services,

Milton, Florida.

Cover Design by Ryan Prucker

Photograph by Sam Montgomery

ISBN 978-1-936513-87-1

2014

TABLE OF CONTENTS

FOREWORD

In order to fully appreciate your PASS experiences, you must FAIL tests along the way.

Failing tests does not always equal failure. Some say experience is the best teacher. If that is the case, then LIFE is the hardest class with the most challenging syllabus and final exams imaginable. What to do next? Will I succeed? Why am I even trying? Does it matter?

LIFE students exchange these questions and many more. Often times we are so consumed by LIFE that we forget to live and dream. One student posed another question, "Should I Live My Dreams?" This student's name is Ronald Mitchell. This book gives a resonating answer to that question through his life. In today's society, the concept of leadership is often associated with status, titles, and political/group affiliation. I believe leadership is also the capacity to translate dreams into reality. Ron's inspirational message of hope, courage, and perseverance will change your life. Enjoy the book and be prepared to look at LIFE in a new way.

Earon Williams Esq.

PROLOGUE

In my own career, a man of very modest means has been able to, through unparalleled efforts, overcome many obstacles. In most cases, many suggest that some progress has been made. In my opinion, it is all too small when considering the day-to-day poverty and pain to which the children throughout the world are subjected.

To everyone who has impacted my life, both positively and negatively, I am grateful for the experiences because they have influenced the person that I am today. I would not change a thing.

Thanks.

ACKNOWLEDGEMENTS

I want to say a heartfelt thanks to all those who have inspired me to share my story and vision with the world. Your support has fueled my personal journey. A special thanks to my mother, grandmother, brothers, sisters, and close friends for their unmatched support and contributions to my life.

INTRODUCTION

I give all credit, glory, and praise to my Lord, Heavenly Father and savior Jesus Christ. The writing of this book was in the living of my life, and putting everything down on paper has been a journey that I never expected to experience. Reliving the past through the scribblings you find here has floated me on emotional clouds, and at the same time dragged me through the muddy valleys. I've been forced to think about people and situations that I had stuffed into the back portions of my brain for years, but in the end, releasing all the negative energy has been therapeutic. The happier times have been a joy to write about, and I couldn't place a value on all the smiles that have wrinkled my cheeks throughout the process.

Getting Jeremie involved was an interesting story in and of itself. I met him in the gym I frequent, and we got to talking. After he mentioned his passion for writing, I got a feeling about him, one of those absolutely certain feelings. I knew he had to be the one to help me deliver my message. I've always been the talker, and all I needed was someone to help organize my words and convey the things I needed to say. The more we talked, the more that feeling was confirmed. Despite what I knew, time was against us. Jeremie was planning a cross-country bicycle trip (with an organization called Bike & Build) and had to leave by June. I met him in late February or early March of 2013, and his trip was scheduled for early June. I had done some writing for the book, but I had a long ways to go. Still, through his training and working, we were able to complete this manuscript before he left. I've come to realize that life is all about the little happenings that you never expect. I'm grateful to have met him and appreciate all the hard work he put into helping me get this book finished.

As you read through these pages I ask a couple of things of you. First, understand that every word I have used, every memory I have shared, is as accurate as I can get it. No one's recollection is perfect, and if I left out a word or situation, I apologize. There may be times when the things that I write sound conceited or cocky, but nothing could be further from the truth. It has never been, and never will be my intention to brag or put myself on a pedestal. All credit for success falls entirely upon God, and I know that without Him none of this thing we call life would be possible. So please do not look at me and think *wow*! Look up when you think that.

Second, this book was created to help others. If you read these pages and do not gain something beneficial, please share it with someone who can. My hope is that the message buried beneath this stack of black and white will be uncovered and spread around the face of this planet. If it can help one person, I will call it a success. If you are not that one, find them and help them.

I can't wait to see the amazing things that you accomplish with your life. Embrace the hunger to succeed and let it fuel you. Make it your mission, your passion, and your driving force. You are the man in the wilderness hunting to survive. The only thing coming between you and your dreams is the Grim Reaper, and even he may not be able to stop you. Your hunger will get you through the tough times. Your hunger will motivate you. Your hunger will motivate someone else. Regardless of what else it does, your hunger will make you successful. If you see nothing else I write, see this: No matter what, you gotta get hungry and stay hungry!

ONE

In the Beginning

A product of poverty and inequality, my mother Elizabeth Mitchell was one of two children born to Robert and Minnie Mitchell. As the granddaughter of a slave, my mother started picking cotton the moment she started walking. Cotton picking was the way of life for African Americans in the south, and sharecropping was the normal means of feeding your family.

She was born on April 28, 1935, and raised on a farm in Oxford, Mississippi. Her parents also picked cotton, and to help make ends meet my grandmother worked as a cook and domestic servant for wealthy Caucasian families. Despite her lack of resources and poor living conditions, my mother had a passion for education and she loved learning.

When she was not working in the cotton field to help support her family, she walked ten miles a day to attend a small, one-room shack that masqueraded as a school. Through hard work and perseverance, my mother became the first in her family to learn how to read and attend and finish high school. This inspired many in my family, including myself, to dream big. It was a beacon of hope and opportunity for so many that came after her.

Like many Americans, my mother supported the civil rights movement, speaking out on several occasions against injustice. One traumatic day while she was walking back from school, she witnessed the twisted face and snapped neck of an African American hanging from a maple tree. This experience could have killed her spirit, but instead it fueled her to support change and seek a better life.

Throughout history, and particularly during the 40s, 50s and 60s in Mississippi, most African Americans were afraid to speak out against any type of unlawful act against them because they knew doing so positioned them for severe and fatal consequences. Despite a great work ethic, she often complained about working in the sweltering sun for twelve to sixteen hours every day only to receive little pay. My mother was a loving and loyal person with a passion for fishing and hunting. She was popular within her community, and well-liked because of her upbeat personality and fighting spirit.

My mother and aunt, Mary Reynolds, often shared their frustration about the unforgiving living conditions in Mississippi and her passion for change. One day, after picking cotton for twelve hours, my mother met with the owner of the cotton farm, Mr. Pat Baker, about the wages paid to her dad. As recalled by my aunt, my mother was in the process of weighing a barrel of cotton when she noticed the scale was broken, and thus they could not receive ample compensation for their labor. Situations like this were well-known facts to many sharecroppers; however, no one had the courage to speak out because they feared for their lives. But my mother, a teenager at this time, inquired about the broken scale after an obvious incorrect weighing. An assistant of Mr. Baker suggested that the scale reading was still accurate. Always the resilient one, she insisted in a polite way that the money received was far less than what she should have been receiving because the scale was faulty. After expressing her frustration multiple times, a new scale was utilized to weigh the barrels of cotton.

For many years my mother continued speaking out against injustice, literally resorting to fisticuffs at times, to defend others that lacked the intestinal fortitude to stand up. Because of her willingness to do what it took to protect the needs of the unable, she earned the nickname Duke, which was rare for a female during this period of time. Because of her growing frustration with her environment, and because of the poor conditions, she was urged to move to Chicago. Everyone agreed the Windy City would be safer and a springboard for a new life.

In Mississippi, my mother witnessed and experienced racism and hatred paralleling that of what Dr. Martin Luther King experienced throughout his fight for equality and justice. As a result she eventually yielded and fled to Chicago. Her voyage became part of the great migration and took place during the middle of the twentieth century.

> **Tears of my Hard Work...are enough to fill the Ocean of my Dreams...**
> — **Shashank Rayal**

Along with my mother, more than six million job-seeking African Americans moved from the rural south into the northern industrial cities. Like my mother, many of them settled in Chicago, and by the 1960s more black Americans lived there than anywhere in the nation. Chicago was appealing to so many because it boasted a lack of the harsh racism that they had been accustomed to throughout the south. Chicago's south side replaced Harlem as the black Mecca of America, and the area cultivated Black Nationalism's political power and ideas. Chicago's black community was like many of the immigrants in other parts of the world, searching for a new identity with a new group of people. For the most part Chicago was and is racially divided by neighborhoods.

Blacks were forced to live in certain areas on the southern side of the city, which caused an influx of people and overcrowding. As a result of the conditions, crime skyrocketed, shops closed down, recreational services dropped and school quality plummeted. There was minimal law enforcement, youth began to take over the streets and gangs like the Black P. Stone Rangers and the East Side Black Disciples were created. Kids in the neighborhoods across the city were being victimized and forced to join a gang to survive. Hundreds of young people were being raised in a multigenerational household where there was no male presence. For those growing up in an urban area, it was common to have never met your father, or to have met him but have no contact with him.

My mother met Fred Jackson, my father, a few years after she had settled down in Chicago. The two instantly hit it off and began to have a short-lived love affair. During this period of time he was married and had five children. My mother was not aware of his marital status at first, and his attraction to her figure and her alluring personality kept his lips sealed. Being the hopeless romantic type, she fell head over heels for him. His previous ties to Mississippi deepened his love for her, as any mutually shared past might. He was a caring, kind, and overall nice guy with presence and movie-star looks. Their bond deepened by the fact they were both at a point in their lives when they were searching for something that had eluded them for many years. They sought the unimaginable, made an intimate choice, and were forever linked together as parents of twin boys. The way I viewed my father was like looking at the silhouette of sunshine buried

> You can't put a limit on anything. The more you dream, the farther you get...
>
> - Michael Phelps

in the clouds during the peak of dawn. I sat and waited for that brilliant moment when it would peek over the barriers and grace me.

When I was a little boy I often asked my mother about my father. I wanted to know more about my heritage. She would often say, "I am your mother *and* father." As I got older I rarely asked her about his existence, but one day I asked about him and she replied, "What do you want to know about him?" Surprised by her answer, I immediately said I wanted to meet him because knowing my family would help prevent me from getting married to a woman that happens to be my sister (I know it sounds odd, but it happens). She said that it had been years since they spoke, but if their paths crossed he would be informed about my interest to meet. She was a wise woman and never said anything negative about him. Although their relationship was a disappointment, she didn't try to poison my mind with any negative images about him. She allowed me time to get to know him and draw my own conclusions. It was a very kind gesture and sacrifice on her behalf,

> I believe that behind every closed door there is an open space...
>
> - Ping Fu

and I respectfully admire how she handled the situation with grace and love.

I met my father for the first time in my early 30s. Our introduction was during a difficult time in my life. I had recently lost my grandmother to Alzheimer's disease and was still healing from the pain I endured watching her die over a period time. Over the years I have gotten to know him and we have managed to build a solid relationship. Although he was absent for the first thirty-two years of my life, he apologized for not being present. Throughout my life I have experienced a lot of hardships and adversity due to my father's absence. I wasn't afforded many of the opportunities and resources that most kids my age (outside of where I lived) were accustomed to, which created many challenges from the moment I was born.

The only male presence within the home was my twin brother, Rodney. Though we were twins, he describes me as more of a mentor to him, and that's how it was growing up. There was no one to teach me how to do basic things like standing up to urinate, how to shave the right way, how to tie a tie, or simply how to be a man, which was especially tough around puberty. The streets were an open door away, so the pimps, the drug dealers and the other negative role models were all that I knew.

Although I loved my mother and grandmother, and admired their tenacity, I was often confronted with situations that required tough decisions. The support of a father was needed. I had to fight physically, mentally and emotionally nearly every day to survive. Only an adult male can teach a boy how to become a man. The pressures and stresses I endured in the streets and at home were sometimes unbearable. It was constantly a kill-or-be-killed environment. Everyone fought, and every little event was fuel to start a fight! The atmosphere reminded me of a mob of pit-bulls trapped in a cage with a couple of steaks between them. If you didn't fight, you didn't survive, at least until you earned some sort of acclaim or respect for yourself. If you didn't fight, the title of "punk" or "sissy" would be hung around your neck and everyone would attack you even more. With that in mind, you always fight. No questions. Just assault. Verbal or physical.

My desire was always to avoid violence when possible, and there were times when I would have to run to the grocery store to prevent robberies, sometimes sprinting as far as six blocks. My grandmother often said that I'd better come back with the groceries, robbers or not, and her words acted like coals under my feet. Some days, I think I barely touched the ground I was moving so fast. If the robbers caught me, I would have to deal with them *and* my grandmother when I got home. Situations like that created a failure-isn't-an-option mindset, and forged my personality in steel.

I love my mother, and I have no regrets about my upbringing, but my mother was a tough woman. I was terrified of her. I knew her rigid rearing was because she loved us, though she never verbalized it to me as a child, and if she didn't keep us straight we would be drowned by the streets. Still, her treatment stained hatred on my heart for a time. Verbally, she would curse me for the smallest grievance. Her cursing of me was so severe that my mind normalized the words and I eventually responded to them like they were my real names. She was the first person to tell me that I would never succeed, and that I would end up like a statistic. Treatment like that made life a cage within a cage. I had to endure the pit-bull cage outside, and then a bear inside the home. I didn't fear the police or the gangs, I feared my mother.

My cousin, Pale Reynolds, was incarcerated when I was younger. When I was twelve years old, my mother took me to see him in prison, and when we left she would say if I ever ended up behind bars she would not come to visit. Rough? Yes. Brutal? Yes. But it was her way of keeping me out of jail.

If I did something that warranted a beating, my grandmother had first dibs. She would tell me to go outside, grab a switch from a tree, and bring it to her so she could beat me with it. If my mother wasn't home when my grandmother was finished, my grandmother reminded me that when my mother came home I would get the second beating, and that's the one I dreaded. If I was already asleep by the time she made it home, she would wake me up, drag me out of bed and tell me to pull down my underpants before thrashing my backside. One time, she told me to take a hot bath after a whipping with a switch, but the hot water wasn't enough. She poured rubbing alcohol into the tub to make things burn even more, and then said I couldn't cry. All that pain, and nowhere for it to go but down into my heart. Going through that will make you tough. I was conditioned emotionally, physically, mentally and verbally and it allowed me to function without a problem out on the street. The pressures and fears of living in the hood didn't faze me as much as they should have. I regret to admit that I could see a woman getting beaten with a bat, kicked and hurt, and I could keep walking. Violence and pain were my every day.

I once made a statement that my mother did not like. She quoted the overused, "I brought you into this world, and I will take you out," phrase, but she took it a step further. She grabbed her rifle, and with a dead serious glisten in her eyes said, "Don't make me use it." I remember seeing the slick black of that rifle and thinking *wow*. That changed my life. How could I not be scared of a woman that brandished a rifle and threatened to kill me if I made her mad? It was that fear that steered me away from gangs, selling drugs, robbing and stealing. I was no angel, but fear kept me out of hell.

Hate trickled down from all the fear. Hate from how

I felt around her, hate from knowing she was serious about ending me if I made her life tougher than it already was, and hate from never experiencing a hug or a kiss from her. There was no balance of affection. Can you imagine how that made me feel? The first time she said that she loved me was when she was ill (when I was an adult), and she never showed affection prior to the sickness. Still, I don't regret a single curse she heaped on my head, a single threat she shook my heart with, or a single beating that whelped my backside. Inside, the bear was brutal, but outside, the pit-bulls didn't seem as vicious. Her treatment allowed me to know that I could handle whatever the world threw at me. Later, she told me she *was* so harsh to keep fear in my heart so that I would stay out of trouble, and boy did it work.

I loved my mother, but growing up I liked my grandmother more because of the affection she showed. She could be tough, as well, but she allowed some soft to filter through her shell. Every so often, she forced me to cook with her, and she showed her love through the food. She let me taste the cake, or the pie, or the chicken, and this created a special feeling for her. It became the way I felt love.

My older sister Pamela (five years older than me and the oldest of the lot) also played a huge role in my development. Aside from being our part-time mother, it was her job to make sure that none of us got into any trouble when we were outside and still relatively young. She did the best she could to shelter us. When I was nine a gang member kicked me off my bike and stole it. Bike jackings weren't uncommon, but my sister wasn't having it happen to her family.

Of course, she grew up in the same environment I did, so naturally she was tough. She found the gang member, beat him up and brought back my bike, saying, "Don't ever let anyone take anything from you."

Even my younger sister, Kim, fought a lot because she had to. I remember her fighting another little girl on one occasion, and people crowded around the scuffle, betting money on who would win. Seeing other people bet on my sister wasn't abnormal because it happened all the time. It was acceptable and okay. My mother gave birth to four children: Pamela, Ronald, Rodney and Kimberly. Both of my sisters had different fathers.

As I reflect upon my life, I wonder how different things would have been if my father was present. I made so many mistakes because I didn't have the proper guidance. Today, I am grateful to have met him. He has helped further my evolution as a man. Additionally, he has imparted some wisdom on me and openly shared with me his failures as a man to ensure that I didn't make the same mistakes. My father was born in a small town in Mississippi called Natchez, where he worked alongside his family picking tobacco and cotton on a farm to help support his eleven siblings. While on the farm he developed a strong work ethic and passion for education. Also migrating to Chicago to seek better employment opportunities, he fortunately found employment as a construction worker, which he did for nearly thirty-five years while serving the community as a volunteer at several local churches.

My dad fathered a total of seven wonderful children: Greg, Bobby, Marion, Trent, Diane, Ronald and Rodney. My parents were never married. They share only twin boys together, but also an abiding faith in the possibilities of this nation. A few months after my mother gave birth to us, my grandfather held us in his arms and began to pray. He looked into our eyes and saw hope and believed that his dreams had come true. Inspired by my grandfather, Robert Mitchell, my mom named us Ronald and Rodney Mitchell. My grandfather was a visionary and believed that America would change for the better one day, and that your skin color would not be a barrier to success.

My grandparents only attained a third grade education, and both imagined their grandchildren attending the best schools in the land, even though they weren't wealthy, because in a God-fearing America you don't have to be wealthy to achieve your potential. They believed that if you wanted to change America you had to master things that don't cost money (like hard work, enthusiasm, passion, innovation and a good attitude) to combat the harsh conditions brought on by segregation, racism and poverty. They lived by this philosophy and passed it down to their children and grandchildren.

My mother and grandparents are all gone now. Yet, I know that they are looking down on me with great pride. Similar to my grandparents' philosophy, one thing my mother instilled in me is that if I wanted to change the world, the change must start within me. If I wanted to make the world a better place, I must first make myself a better man. I had to become a beacon of hope for the less fortunate and lost to look to. Her words came when I was already an adult, but it still changed my outlook on life. It gave me a deeper appreciation for her and the man she was trying to make me through her version of rearing. I'd always respected her, but after her inspiration, I tried my hardest to treat her like royalty and she responded to it in a positive way.

Their spirits live on and I am grateful for their hard work and sacrifice, aware that my grandparents' and parents' dreams thrive through my family. I acknowledge that my story is part of the larger American story, and that I owe a great debt to all of those who came before me, and that, in no other place on earth, is my story even possible. The unimaginable is now a reality.

TWO

Urban Ambition

Chicago - the tough streets on the South Side

6414 WOODLAWN

Tucked away in a small corner, deep in the heart of Chicago's South Side, is Woodlawn Avenue: A place where I spent my childhood and learned how to survive a gang, drug and rat-infested environment. Woodlawn stretched about fifteen miles long. Abandoned buildings were more prevalent than the occupied ones. Drugs and drug transactions were everywhere and dope needles peppered the ground. One could see addicts shooting up and smoking crack on church steps, and it wasn't any more peculiar than watching a man drink a can of coke.

I grew up at 6414 South Woodlawn Avenue: a grooming ground and pit-stop for pimps, prostitutes, players, hustlers, gamblers, drug-dealers, killers and notorious gangs. The building itself had three floors and twelve units, six on either side of a courtyard. Throughout my building, lingering and varying in strength depending

17

upon the temperature and the wind's direction, there was a putrid odor seeping through walls, doors and windows, despite how tight they were bolted together. Certain parts of the landscape were barren and devoid of people, populated instead with toxins like rusted batteries, shredded tires, broken glass and nails. Prior to moving to Woodlawn Avenue, my mother lived with her sister, Mary, in the Robert Taylor Homes (a low-income housing development) for a few years until she was able to secure better employment. After leaving her sister, she took up residence in the apartment that I called home until I became twenty-two-years old.

The inside of the apartment was rather large, consisting of four small bedrooms, a kitchen with a pantry, a living room, a dining room and one bathroom. Our apartment was immaculate the majority of the time; however, it was not enough to combat living in an overcrowded building and community. The floors were covered with cheap tile to conceal the many holes and corrosion. Our ceiling was eventually splattered with grease spots created from the heat and many hours my grandmother spent cooking three meals every day for years (my grandmother moved to Chicago from Oxford, Mississippi to live with us shortly after my grandfather

Robert Mitchell died). Adjacent to the grease spots were several cracks in the ceiling, a result of water leaking from pipes.

There were iron heaters located in every room to keep us warm during the harsh winters. Unfortunately, at the bottom of nearly every heater there were small holes alongside the pipes. The holes became increasingly larger due to nibbling rats that begin to eat through the tile, allowing their cronies from the street to enter into our home. Throughout the night I could hear, and sometimes see, rats dashing from one room to another. Sometimes, they would even climb onto my blanket and dance across my bed in the middle of the night. The first time it happened I was afraid, but it became a reoccurring event, and over the years I grew accustomed to the fact that my bed was a playground for rats.

My grandmother often made us help her clean up and assigned us chores like taking out the garbage, washing the walls and sweeping the floor. This made us accountable for our actions and gave us a sense of ownership to ensure that we would take good care of our home and property.

As a teenager, I didn't like to clean and quite often complained to anyone that would listen. I once confided in a junkie about how hard things were in my life.

"Life can be a wonderful experience, if you approach the good and bad days with the same attitude," he said, scratching his thigh. "You're a good kid, shrewd, unlike your friends. You're one of the trustworthy ones around here." He started smiling as he continued. "I know you work as a caddie up at Jackson's, you have a paper route and you bag groceries for the old folk over at Vito's." His eyes turned cold and serious as he went on.

> **Those who stop when it's tough will never get to the top...**
>
> **- Oludare Oduale**

"Don't be like me, kid. Stay away from dope and stay in school. It'll help you go places and see the world." He held out a grungy hand that was thick and ashy around the knuckles. I took it, giving it a firm shake without any hesitancy. "You've got a bright future. Use your mind as the tool for every problem. No bullets or blades."

He essentially conveyed that no matter how difficult the circumstances are, if I didn't mind or really fear the outcome, I could find a solution and overcome any situation (FYI, Vito's was a local grocery store and Jackson's was Jackson Park Golf Course).

"Thanks. Why are you homeless? Are you married with children?"

"Yeah," he looked away, scratching his track-lined forearm. "Got three little ones."

"Where are they?"

After my words his glare was cold and empty. "Have a good day, kid. Stay out of trouble. We need people like you to help change this crazy world."

That was the only conversation we had, but over the years I saw him eating out of the garbage and collecting bottles and beer cans. I asked a neighbour what happened to him, and she replied that he was once an excellent student; however, he started hanging out with the wrong people. Eventually, he dropped out of high school and began to use and sell drugs. He was later convicted and went to prison for the attempted murder of a man who was his best friend. One evening they were getting high together and he begin hallucinating, thinking that his best friend was a demon pursuing him. He beat up his best friend and nearly killed him, in addition to injuring another innocent bystander. Upon release from prison, he could not find employment and eventually lost hope and the will to live. Now he was homeless and a drug addict. It was depressing to learn that he had endured such a tough time.

Stories like his are all too familiar in America today, and much can be tied to the dropout rate of the youth. Every year, 1.3 million American students, seven thousand a day, drop out of school. General Colin Powell of America's Promise Alliance said, "It is not just a crisis, it is a catastrophe." Poor students, minorities and those in the South have the highest rates. The U.S. government has identified several low-performing schools across America that produce nearly half of the nation's dropouts. President Obama calls them "Dropout Factories" and wants to shut them down, or turn them into charter schools. "You can't defend a status quo in which a third of our kids are dropping out," said President Obama. Some believe that it takes a village to raise a child, and I think it will take a nation to educate our students.

THE WEDGEWOOD

The building next to my complex was an eleven-story hotel that had been converted into a housing project for low-income people. The Wedgewood Hotel was located one block from 63rd street at the intersection of Woodlawn, 64th, and Minerva in the Woodlawn neighborhood. At one time the hotel was owned in part by Jesse Owens, and sported bigwig residents like Joe Louis and Minnie Minoso. The El Rukn gang, an Islamic faction of the Black P. Stone Nation, was the hotel's last owner.

The Wedgewood was approximately twenty feet north of the building where my apartment was located. It occupied 1/4 of a city block in length, looked like a U.S. Navy battle ship, and was more notorious than other low-income housing projects like Cabrini Green and the Robert Taylor Holmes (where I also frequented as a teen because many of my cousins lived there). The Wedgewood was a dangerous but fun place because it was filled with hundreds of children. I spent a lot of time there playing with kids, or picking up and delivering groceries for elder residents. I often walked from the first floor to the eleventh floor since the elevators were out of service. On the eleventh floor, I hung out by the fire escape, and sneaked onto the roof of the Wedgewood whenever I could. I always enjoyed viewing the epic Chicago skyline from up there.

Looking down from the roof, human beings looked more like ants. I was exposed to a new world and witnessed several crimes. I saw police officers chasing suspects through alleys and gang members gathering to plot their next crime. I saw junkies robbing people at gun point for money to buy drugs, and other people overdosing on drugs. I saw women being beaten up, sold by pimps, and even being raped. I saw police officers rob drug dealers, and drug dealers rob apartments during different times of the day. I saw many people commit suicide by jumping from the seventh, eighth and ninth floor apartment windows (usually a result of the influx of drugs). It happened so frequently that sometimes I took chalk and created a mock crime scene. Needless to say, the long line of police cars, ambulances, dead bodies and pools of blood on the street no longer affected me. Looking down from the rooftop of the Wedgewood provided me with the ultimate blueprint and *how-to strategies* to avoid trouble, problem solve and function in a dangerous environment.

Adding to what I saw from the roof, I learned more about problem solving through interactions with my brothers and sisters than any institution of higher learning I ever attended. My sister Pamela is the oldest of four, and we are five years apart in age. Throughout my childhood my mother worked long hours, and my grandmother made Pam responsible for our well-being because our neighborhood was so dangerous, and we were too small and weak to defend ourselves. As I touched on before, she was street smart, fearless and able to handle herself in lieu of dangerous circumstances (much like most young African Americans that grew up in such hostile environments). For years, I watched my sister protect me from neighborhood predators and beat up boys like she was a Roman warrior. Although she was attractive, she also had a mean left hook like Mike Tyson.

My grandmother taught us that if one of us ever got into a fight and we didn't help, we would be severely punished. My sister didn't lose many fights because it was unacceptable. I admire her courage and willingness to fight our battles as a youth. Today, our approaches to problem solving bare little similarities; however, I love and respect her strength as a person. Faced with insurmountable odds, she rose to the challenge on numerous occasions. Like my grandmother, Pamela's vision was a catalyst for change. Her leadership helped to provide a better life and living conditions for my mother and every member of my family. Her efforts cannot be measured. They blazed a trail for many, including myself.

My sister Kimberly is the youngest of my siblings, and like my mother, is a devoted and giving person. As a youth she fought other girls in our neighborhood to survive and gain respect. Although she did not like to fight, she too overcame many obstacles. I admire her endurance, personality and intellect. Kim embodies an unmatched focus and determination. I watched her work two or three jobs for many years to pay her college tuition. Although she was subjected to poverty and limited resources, she refused to follow many of her friends and become a mother as a teenager. I love Kim. She has become an example and not a statistic. She is an inspiration for many women.

Today, I share a special bond with my brother Rodney. As children we often fought and competed against each other, but he is the epitome of kindness, grace and humility. Unfortunately, Rodney has multiple sclerosis and was misdiagnosed a child. Because of this he suffered physically for many years. A student of the moment, he has inspired me to be the best that I can be and to live my dreams, no matter what. I love Rodney. He personifies strength. He never gave up on life and refused to allow his illness define his future. All my siblings have experienced different forms of adversity. They taught me how to use an unfavorable experience as a stepping-stone to overcome my past and embrace the future.

As a kid, the view from the Wedgewood was like being on top of the world. It taught me a lot about the three Cs of life: common sense, common knowledge and common practice. I learned that it was important to meet people where they are in their life and in the moment we share together. For example: whenever I visit sick individuals in hospitals, seniors in retirement homes, or speak to young children, I always squat down so I can look at them square in the eye before I begin to speak. It is a simple method I use to establish an instant connection, creating a friendly and nurturing environment. In most cases it helps to create a unique line of communication, a meeting within the moment that embodies that special instant when two minds connect for the first time. Effective communication is necessary to problem solve, build relationships, inspire and educate.

Common sense suggests that without it we cannot function properly in society. Additionally, I learned that common knowledge in an urban environment is not common for mainstream America. Although there are a few similarities between the two, the majority of knowledge that most people acquire will likely be dictated by their experiences and level of exposure.

One day while I was on top of the Wedgewood looking down on the world, I saw a lady get her purse snatched. The lights had been turned off because a drug transaction was in process. It was common knowledge that when the lights were turned off in a particular area, something bad was about to happen. If you were not familiar with my neighborhood, you could easily find yourself in this hazardous situation. I'm convinced that the lady that got her purse snatched did not live in my community. If she was native to the area she would not have been walking alone down a pitch-black street at night.

An example of common knowledge is when, in a drug infested area, you witness a person walking down the street with a long winter jacket on during the summer time. If you see this, it's likely that the individual is caring a firearm and is in the process of committing an act of violence. I was exposed to a lot of invaluable information looking down from the Wedgewood; however, the most vital part of what I learned is common practice: implementing something that is viewed by a group of people as common sense and common knowledge.

A common sense example is a person studying the necessary information before an examination and knowing this will improve his chances of getting a good grade; additionally, common knowledge dictates that practice makes perfect. Although this philosophy is widely accepted by most people in America, it is still not common practice.

My mother often directed me to do something, and

before I did it, she would ask me three questions. Did it make sense? Do you know exactly what was being required of you? If I responded yes, she then asked me if I was ready. In other words, if it makes sense and you know what to do, then do it.

Although I have traveled throughout the world and experienced a lot from home and abroad, the most transferable skill that I learned is how to influence others through communication. In my neighborhood, verbal and non-verbal language were used to spearhead drug transactions, steal, commit robberies, identify undercover police officers, instill fear in the heart of a man without speaking one word, and convey power and strength by using body language to make statements.

An old childhood friend that had been incarcerated for many years once told me that you can tell if an inmate had been locked up for the first time if you watch their body language and eye contact. He also said that if the inmate displayed any fear, he immediately became prey and a target for extortion or rape. Unfortunately, this was also true on the streets. I witnessed many childhood friends get beaten up, ridiculed, threatened and made the poster child for weakness because they refused to fight or defend themselves. I learned first-hand that having the respect of your peers and enemies is just as important as being loved by them. The same people that celebrate you one day can and will destroy or harm you the next day. The people that respect you will most likely not hurt you.

On several occasions I witnessed the power of respect, but one day during a summer league basketball tournament a gang member named Smoke was in my neighborhood for a game. He was a member of the Black P. Stones. The game was being played in rival gang territory. Typically, if you were caught in such a situation, you would be beaten up and left for dead. However, he was a dynamic basketball player and carried himself like a warrior. He didn't fear anyone, and whenever he played basketball he attacked the basket aggressive enough, and dunked the basketball hard enough, that you thought he was trying to tear down the rim. His approach to the game was like Lebron James, and just like the King, he was as fearless and strong as an ox. As a result he was allowed to play without problems. His body language and presence on and off the court forced rival gang members to rethink their position and strategy and not cause him trouble. His position certainly wasn't hindered by his carrying a gun at all times, or his lack of fear to use it.

Behind the Wedgewood was a senior citizen home

for low-income seniors located on Minerva Avenue. Directly behind the senior citizen home was James Wadsworth Elementary School.

WADSWORTH ELEMENTRY SCHOOL

Wadsworth elementary school is the Chicago public school that I attended K through eighth grade. During my nine years as a student, I experience academic hardship and multiple emotional, physical and psychological challenges as a result of my social and economic environment.

As I reflect on the past I realize there were also many awesome moments shared with the senior citizens in my community. Screaming at us to stay off their lawns, the seniors sat outside and frequently watched us rip and run through their manicured grass, begging us to just use the sidewalk instead. Between fits of frustration and lawn repair, they often stopped us and tried to impart the wisdom that they had acquired throughout their lives. They observed us walk to and from Wadsworth elementary school every day for years, and as a result saw our maturation and growth. As we aged they allowed us to play football on their grass just to keep us out of trouble. Many simply had compassion because they knew we turned vacant lots into baseball and football fields. These lots were filled with dirt, weeds and old needles used by drug addicts. Even worse, the nearby buildings were not only abandoned and burned down, but were known to be occupied by dead bodies.

Wadsworth was a familiar territory for two of America's most notorious gangsters, Larry Hoover and Jeff Fort. Larry Hoover was the leader of the Black Gangster Disciples Nation and Fort, aka the Angel of Death, was the leader of the Black P. Stone Nation. Wadsworth, like many other Chicago public schools, was a feeder system for the Department of Illinois Corrections. Their influence caused Wadsworth to be the dividing territory for the two largest Chicago gangs. Everything located to the west of Woodlawn belonged to the Black Gangster Disciples Nation, and everything east of Woodlawn was Black P. Stone Nation territory. Each year, more than one hundred students matriculate from Wadsworth to Hyde Park Career Academy high school. In spite of limited resources, Wadsworth was the launching pad for talented athletes, dancers, entertainers, leaders, politicians and successful entrepreneurs.

Because of increasing gang activity, everyone I knew was affiliated with a gang. If you weren't it was impossible to survive. I wasn't, and didn't dare to be, because of my mother, so I had to pretend in order to get by. I can't explain it as any more than an act of God, but I was able to avoid a lot of the gang activity. I could pose and people left me alone without ridicule or question. Everyone knew I could fight, and I knew everyone, yet no one seemed to notice that I wasn't actually in a gang even though I acted in ways that suggested otherwise.

Like all academic institutions, Wadsworth had its young gifted students, but it was also a breeding ground for violence, teenage pregnancy and high school drop-outs. There were some outstanding students and amazing teachers working at Wadsworth. Sadly, their efforts were not capitalized upon due to an out-dated educational system.

Many kids were awarded diplomas in eighth grade because of social promotion, which afforded them the opportunity to attend high schools. Social promotion is the practice of passing a student (usually a general education student, rather than a special education student) to the next grade at the end of the current school year, regardless of whether they learned the necessary material, in order to keep them with their peers by age (that being the intended social grouping). It is sometimes referred to as promotion based on seat time, or the amount of time the child spent sitting in school. Many supporters of social promotion believe that promotion is done in order not to harm the students' or their classmates' self-esteem, to encourage socialization by age, to facilitate student involvement in sports teams, or to promote a student who is weak in one subject on the basis of strength in the other areas. Unfortunately, this was and is still a reoccurring event in the Chicago public school systems and across America. The majority of my classmates began high school with reading and math skills on a fourth, fifth and sixth-grade level as a result of social promotion.

The educational resources provided to me during my upbringing were aligned with the educational strategy that governed my school. In fourth grade I recall writing over my sister Pamela's name in an English and social studies book. Pamela used the same two books five years earlier when she was in the fourth grade. This was a familiar experience for African-American students attending public schools within the city. Tragically, the parents of students who resided in poor neighborhoods paid fewer taxes, and as a result their children received less funding. If you pay more taxes and reside in a more affluent environment, then your child's school was likely to receive more funding. Because of this, your child was likely to acquire the necessary tools to compete in the global, academic war. Moreover, the type of educational system we endured was a pipeline to some of the most well-known

> Self-discipline, high self-esteem, self-confidence, self-motivation and hard work are essential in order to succeed in life...
>
> - Author Unknown

institutions in the country like Joliette, Statesville and Pontiac State prisons, opposing the well-known institutions of higher education like Harvard, Yale and Stanford University, that children of affluent descent would be more positioned to attend.

Many educators believe that my educational experience was under-funded, which caused several passionate and talented teachers to be frustrated, (and this was exasperated by the fact that they were underpaid and over-worked). The lack of resources provided to African-American students leaves many unprepared for high school.

Adding insult to injury, the curriculum used throughout the school year did not mirror the information on standardized tests. Quite naturally, whenever I took a standardized examination I performed very poorly. The majority of the information that I was tested on was foreign, and to me it was like reading Chinese. These tests were given annually, and I knew before I sat down to take the examinations that I had failed. Nearly eighty-five percent of my peers experienced the same frustration that I did when the standardized test was given. It was a no-win situation. We were being set up to fail. However, our white counter parts were positioned to do well and advance academically.

THE COMMUNITY AND BASEBALL, YMCA

After the northern migration of African Americans from the South, the Chicago of the 1960s and 70s was a city of racial tension. Rev. Dr. Martin Luther King, Jr. was the word on the street, having visited Chicago on many occasions during the sixties to meet with the late Mayor Richard Daley in an attempt to knock down the walls of racial segregation.

If you lived west of Woodlawn, you were a member of the Black P. Stone Nation led by Jeff Fort. If you lived east of Woodlawn Avenue, you were a member of the Larry Hoover led Black Disciples Nation who ruled the air, streets, and movement of the human spirit. The schoolyard was like a jungle for many people because of the crimes and shooting that took place during and after school hours. As a child, I often heard the rallying cry "Stone run it," which meant the Black P. Stone Nation ran the streets. Gang crimes got so bad that the Chicago police officers created a gang task force to combat the murders.

During the 1960s, T.W.O., a community development organization designed to help improve neighborhoods and youth in Woodlawn, was created. Jeff Fort, the leader of the Black P. Stone Nation, began to work closely with T.W.O., and as a result the organization received a one million dollar job-training grant. Many of the Black P. Stone Nation gang leaders ran the program, which was designed to help kids acquire job training and build the morale of the community; but, the members were terrorizing the community. Subsequently, the program was later dissolved and Jeff Fort was convicted and sent to prison for the mismanagement of grant funds.

As in other northern U.S. cities at the time, there were many things that black people in Chicago couldn't do. In some cases they were still riding on the back of the bus. We weren't allowed to enter certain places through the front door, and we weren't allowed into certain parts of the city during the day, especially after hours. The south side of Chicago was, and still is, made up of mostly black migrants from the South who came to the North in search of jobs in area slaughterhouses and steel mills. I grew up in a world marked block after block with red brick tenements and vacant lots. Poverty and despair were the rule of the day.

Like many kids, I loved to play basketball, baseball and football year round. During the summer, every major street within a two-mile radius (north, south, east and west) started their own baseball, basketball and football teams to compete for street credibility and bragging rights. Though I knew the games were fun and helped pass the time, I didn't realize they would enable me to develop qualities that would serve me well in life. Qualities like sportsmanship, organizing, team building, public speaking and recognition among peers. Unfortunately, many of the teams were comprised of several members from different gangs, which was the motivating factor for several fights during and after the games.

I helped organize some of the games we played, all while lobbying for peace among gang members. My team played against the Kimbark Dodgers, University Pirates and Greenwood Mean Machine three times each throughout the summer, and at least two of those games ended in what we called a free fall. A free fall was a fight that was planned by the team that was at the moment losing. The losing team initiates the free fall to convey their displeasure in losing. At its core, it was a premeditated gang fight camouflaged by a baseball game. Many of my teammates looked forward to a free fall to make a point that they were superior and ruled gang turf.

Since I was present when the fights would break out, I had to get involved to keep face. I had to hit someone, knock them down, fight for a little bit before I could run. If I didn't, the gang I was posing to be a part of wouldn't see my allegiance, and I would become a target.

Though the gangs saturated the neighborhood, I developed many of my leadership skills dealing with them. I learned how to organize people, how to problem solve, how to communicate effectively (though not properly) and how to manipulate, diffuse, or ignite a situation. There was a time when I was playing baseball and another gang came by shouting offensive slurs. The gang I was playing with were rivals with the offenders, and back then all it took was a word to cause a fight. We had two choices: either chase them and fight, or continue playing ball. I decided I wanted to continue playing, so I told my teammates not to worry about the other gang. We could get back at them another way. There was a party that night, so I told them to save their energy for the girls at the party. The method worked, and the continuation of the game probably stopped a shooting, and certainly saved a few kids from going to the hospital. Stuff like that happened all the time, and my dealings with gangs enabled me to discover how to redirect a negative situation toward a favorable outcome.

Gangs were a double-edged sword in my life. They've destroyed countless lives, but they also pushed me to develop as a leader, helping me to nurture positive skills in the most hostile environment. Dealing with killers made the rest of America easy.

YMCA

My dear friend and brother in faith, Arthur Ford, once said, "Adversity doesn't build character, but reveals character." Through my aggregate personal experiences I have found this to be true. One day when I was walking home from the YMCA located on 62nd and Drexel, a teenager approached me from an angle and requested that I give him all my money. I looked at the kid as though he was joking until he raised his gun and pointed it at my head. Initially, I didn't know what to do because I had never been robbed at gunpoint before; however, after pausing for a few seconds to get my composure, I turned and glared past the barrel of the gun and into the hurting eyes of the gunman.

With no fear I said, "I only have a few bucks."

His angered response was, "I am going to ask you one more time. Give me every dime in your pocket right now."

I reached in my pocket and handed him all two dollars and fifty cents of my money. While forking over the little I had, I noticed he had several tattoos on his arm. They were gang symbols that I was familiar with because of the drug and gang-infested environment I was accustomed to. The tattoos let me know that he was a member of the Black Gangster Disciples Nation, which was the largest gang in the country at that time.

"Where are you from?" I asked. "I'm from 63rd and Woodlawn."

63rd and Woodlawn was an area located on the South Side of Chicago, and well-known for giving birth to the famous gang leaders David Barkdale, Larry Hoover and Jeff Fort. Growing up in my neighborhood, you had to become familiar with gang signs, rules, laws and vernacular to survive. Considering the circumstances of being robbed, I presented myself as a member of the Black Gangster

Disciples Nation and began to recite a few gang laws to him to convey that we were a part of the same organization, and that we didn't rob each other. Then I said that he should be getting some real money instead of robbing me, and that I knew where and how to get paid. He paused and asked what money, and prodded me to tell him more. As I did he lowered the gun from my head. I allowed him to keep the money, acting like nothing had happened as we began to talk, even laughing after sharing stories about our respected neighborhoods and gang experiences. My plea for assembly worked. He concealed his gun in the back of his jeans and said "Yeah, let's get this money, dog."

As we continued to talk I learned his name was John. I learned his story and why he decided to rob me for the $2.50 I had in my pocket. Like so many Americans, he was homeless. A drug addict, his mother had been evicted from her home. As a result he had to feed and provide shelter for himself and a younger sibling, and committing such a crime was the only way he believed he could support himself.

He asked me something that I'll never forget: "If you were in my shoes, what would you do?" I explained there was a better way, but he insisted there wasn't and that nobody was going to hire a high school dropout. I maintained that he be patient, and immediately he shouted that he couldn't wait because he needed money to feed himself. I begged to differ and shared with him some historical information about the plight of Americans and what we have overcome and been through. I simply told him, "It is possible." In other words, he could find a job, food, shelter and the support he needed to turn his life around.

I requested that he visit my home one day soon, and if he did I would provide him with some food. I knew my grandmother was a great cook, and she would provide him with some southern hospitality and sustenance. The only string I attached to the offer was that he had to get rid of the firearm. He accepted my terms and invitation.

The more we talked, the more I understood his situation and the more I really wanted to help him. I was overwhelmed with joy when he made good on visiting my home at a time that my grandmother had recently made her famous sweet potato pie. Her pie was so delicious that when you ate it you immediately had to take your shoes off and wiggle your toes. My friends often said that her pie was so good it could end war in foreign countries and bring peace to the world. Thankfully, he made it in time to try a piece.

Inside my home we talked more while my grandmother cooked dinner, and he thanked me again for inviting him over. During dinner my grandmother was impressed with his enormous smile and humble spirit. Because of her southern roots she enjoyed kids with a healthy appetite.

After the meal was over my grandmother prepared an additional plate and a bag of food for him to take along on his journey. As we walked back to the area where I met him,

> **Winning, without the risk of losing, is a feeble victory...**
>
> **- Raymond C. Nolan**

he conveyed that my invitation was the nicest thing anyone had ever done for him, and that he was sorry for attempting to commit such a vicious act of violence. I asked him to make sure that he gave his little brother some of the food that had been prepared. I also made it clear that if he ever needed another meal he would be welcomed in my house.

I reiterated that killing just to feed yourself was not smart, and that he possessed gifts and talents that would allow him to be successful. Additionally, I stated that great things were supposed to happen to him. He laughed and said, "I know what you're going to say 'it's possible' and that everything is going to be okay."

Since that scenario, I can better empathize and sympathize with people. You never know what you will do when put in a position where you have little hope and resources, and when you're in an environment where the attitude of everyone around you is kill or be killed. This experience was confirmation that I could lead and advocate on behalf of others because I had to advocate for my life under duress.

As a result of this experience I discovered that I had several unique gifts. I learned that I possessed a phenomenal ability to problem solve, communicate and lead people to act in a manner that is beneficial to all. Also, I recognized that I could function at a high level under pressure (all types except testing). Sadly, I had to be confronted with such adversity to recognize my gifts and talents. When facing an enormous amount of pressure, as I have on several occasions, a person is forced to give up or fight. Moments like these help build and develop character, strength, courage, tenacity and willpower.

No young person in the greatest country in the world should be subjected to such circumstances. Without basic necessities like food, shelter, education, healthcare, support, love and financial resources, America will continue to produce thousands of kids like John. John was a nice guy, extremely athletic, very articulate, tall and muscular. He possessed a great sense of humour and he liked school; however, due to circumstances that he was confronted with as a child, I was not surprised by the poor choices John made.

Before I lost contact with him we remained in communication for many years. I continued to offer my support whenever I could to help him throughout his journey in life. He eventually received his high school diploma and entered the military to begin to create a better life for himself and his family.

I am grateful that I was able to support John, and he later insisted that I was his guardian angel because I was kind enough to help him despite how he initially treated me. Unfortunately, this is not a familiar ending. Many young people like John lack the intestinal fortitude to turn their lives around. Nearly a hundred of my friends from my neighborhood have been murdered or incarcerated because they have consistently lived a life of crime and violence. John was one of the most important people I've ever met. He confirmed to me that anything is possible.

Millions of young people are being born into a life filled with hardship and struggle that mirrors the darkness of being trapped in a tunnel. Such circumstances create desperate measures and give birth to the worst a human being can offer. To combat this cycle we must provide hope through inspiration, education and innovation. I believe it's possible to live your dreams and soar like an eagle to new heights. I also believe that every human being is born with gifts and talents to improve the communities where they currently live. Additionally, I believe that it's possible to transform our schools, hospitals, streets, playgrounds, libraries and lives. Unfortunately, this change must come at a price that many are not willing to pay. For example: to change our communities we first must change the way we think and process information. We must be willing to do the things that many countries will not do to have the success that others can only hope and imagine achieving. The simplest way to bring about change is through the human spirit.

As a child, my mother often articulated the importance of education and how it is the key to success, opportunity, access and resources, and a springboard for sound decision-making. She believed it would equalize the playing field for minorities and women in America. Although my mother was exposed to a second-class education compared to other Americans, she knew that all education was not equal and that life itself was the best experience and education anyone could ever receive. I was taught that the jewels of life could not be mined in a classroom, and was urged to become a student of life and to master the things that cost no money. Hard work, passion and enthusiasm are good examples of things cultivated from life's struggles because they offer change. It took me years to understand this philosophy. When I was a child, hard work was something I tried to avoid on some occasions, but on other occasions I appreciated it because my mother and grandmother preached that it would increase my intensity level, challenge my endurance and bring the best out of me.

Enthusiasm demands that you have a deep infatuation about a person, thing or opportunity, and you must also be willing to exert yourself for free if needed. On the other hand, passion is a deep desire and a need to accomplish something, a hunger or thirst to act, participate, help, defend and even nurture. As a youth I possessed these characteristics, but didn't recognize the impact it would make on my life as an adult.

Informal education - learning disability, CPS school system, Mr. Pruitt, street smarts

As a product of one of the most notorious gang and drug-infested communities in America, I received two different types of education. The first type of education was traditional. I attended James Wadsworth Elementary School, located at 6410 south University Avenue, approximately two blocks east of my childhood home. I grew up as an average student by Chicago's school standards (B student), but at other schools I would probably have been a D student. I was always being taught two years in the past because the school curriculum was behind. The teachers were wonderful, and many of my fond memories reflect that, but they had limited resources. It was like giving a car to a person with no gas. Pushing the vehicle can only go so far before more is needed.

Like many of my peers, I was passed along through school. Back then, graduating a certain class size meant more money, so teachers would do what they felt was best to help the school succeed overall. Many times, I was passed along but did not deserve to move to the next level, and my experience was the typical. To academically be eighteen months behind was no big deal. Standardized testing was a nightmare. The things on the test simply weren't taught in my classes. They were showing me how to boil pasta in class, but the test was on how to flambé Coq Au Vin. That being my foundation, you can imagine how difficult college and the workforce would be for me. Much of what I lacked started with the resources that I received in school.

All that being said, I loved, and still love, learning. Despite taking five years to graduate, I went to school whenever I could for the most part. From Kindergarten to eighth grade, I received the perfect attendance award. I woke up and trekked through those rough streets every day, even walking through the blizzard of 1979 to reach my education destination. White was everywhere that day, and it took me thirty minutes to go three blocks. I arrived at the school and saw it was closed, but I didn't mind. School was my thing. I loved school because it provided an escape from the rest of my life.

Though I was perfect with my school attendance before high school, sports became more important as I got older. I still loved to learn, but athletes only needed a 1.7 GPA to play. In addition, teachers passed athletes along, which tragically still can happen today. That's how I managed to be a year or two behind where I should have been, maintain a D average my senior year, and graduate with a fifth grade reading level.

Although my formal education was typical in comparison to other urban school systems across America, my informal education was anything but traditional. I attended the school of Hard Knocks and graduated from the University of Street Smarts. The lessons learned there are typically by trial and error, with minimal room for error, and the consequences are often severe and painful. Unlike the traditional format, there are no makeup examinations. It was imperative to be able to survey the environment and to be mobile on your feet. In such a hostile and volatile community, a very dangerous situation could arise at any giving moment. To the detriment of the needy, certain attributes like instinct, common sense, drive and wisdom can't be taught. I believe you can only acquire the preceding qualities through life experiences, constant exposure, or a combination of the two.

One day, I was sauntering toward a bus stop six blocks away from my home when I noticed a man walking fifty yards behind me on the opposite side of the street. As I proceeded my instincts compelled me to look back over my shoulder. That same man was now trotting fifteen feet directly behind me. His right hand was in his coat pocket, and the other hand was inside the upper part of his coat.

This man could have simply been in a hurry, but my street smarts suggested otherwise.

While I power walked I spotted a man approximately twenty-five feet ahead of me. With my options dwindling, I yelled out a random name and jogged toward the distant stranger to catch up with him. The stranger slowed down and glanced over his shoulder. When I got within ten feet I said hello and apologized for mistaking him for someone else. I looked back over my shoulder and the man who was following me had come to a complete stop. We made eye contact, and I smiled, indicating that I knew what he was up to. He nodded his head, acknowledging that my instincts were accurate.

Growing up in such a rough environment acclimated me to being preyed upon by members of my community. As a result I developed a hard shell to survive. Witnessing so many good and innocent people being taken advantage of, harmed and even murdered created a constant state of distrust. I was taught at a very early age to be kind, respectful, sincere and careful because my parents would not always be present to protect me.

*Learning how to lead - breakdancing, gang
experience, Hyde Park high school, etc.*

There were always a lot of mischievous things to get involved with for the youth in my community. I loved, respected and feared my mother enough to stay away from most of those things, so I participated in sports.

Another activity I got involved with was breakdancing. Breakdance, or breaking, is a street-based dance that incorporates intricate body movements, coordination, style and aesthetics. It also entails characteristics similar to gymnastics, karate, ballet and street dance, making it unique and very appealing. Those who perform this style of dance are also known as b-boys or b-girls.

Breakdance is one of the oldest known hip-hop styles of dance, and is believed to have originated in the Bronx, New York in the 1970s. The music used when I performed this art form was inspired by the energetic enactments of the funk maestro, James Brown. According to numerous sources, in the early days of disc jockeys, emcees and b-boys, breaks (instrumental part of a song that is looped repeatedly by the DJ) were incorporated into songs to allow a display of improvised breakdance steps.

Music is a key part of breaking, but hip-hop is not the only option. During the 70's soul, funk and even jazz tunes all worked just as well. Spontaneity, style, fashion, concept and technique are also vital aspects of this art form.

At the tender age of thirteen, I fell in love with breaking and the lifestyle as a street performer and entertainer. At fourteen, despite being named the starting pitcher for the varsity baseball team, I quit to chase my newfound love. I had no idea that it would help me advance my leadership, communication, interpersonal, management, entrepreneurial and negotiation skills. Not to mention it helped keep me out of trouble. Also, I learned how to be disciplined and focused, becoming physically and mentally strong. During my career as an entertainer I spent thousands of hours developing my moves and other skills to become one of the best in the world. Some recognized me as an athlete out on the streets, but more recognized me as a dancer. Though breaking is thought to have started in New York, the people of Chicago loved and respected the people that breakdanced.

While I was a student at Wadsworth Elementary School, I begin to study breakdance along with other kids that lived in the community. One of the kids that danced with me throughout my career was Ronald Bell. I first met

Ronald in the second grade. He was very athletic and fun to be around. We both had a passion for sports; therefore, we played on teams that represented the block we lived on. Quite naturally, we competed against each other all throughout the year. We both gained an enormous amount of respect from our peers as a result of our athleticism and competitive spirit.

Ron looked up to me because he felt I always had everything together, but I looked up to him because of his drive and passion for whatever he was doing. We had a lot in common and similar interest like popping and locking. Experts define "popping" as a street dance, and one of the original funk styles that came from the African-American communities of California during the 60s and 70s. Through many hours of practice, I learned that it was based on the technique of quickly contracting and relaxing muscles to cause a jerk in my body. "Locking" is another funk style based on the concept of locking particular movements after moving fast for a few seconds. Fast and distinct arm and hand movements combined with more relaxed hips and legs may also be required.

We both spent many hours developing our moves and dancing whenever we received an opportunity. As a result, our paths crossed at school and we admired each other's moves and begin performing together with another friend named Mike. Mike was a good dancer and an exceptional football player. The chemistry was solid, but Mike took part in activities that Ronald Bell and I didn't appreciate, things like getting high and gang banging. Therefore, our trio was short lived. Although we liked being around Mike, his morals and values compromised our mission. He left the group after a few months.

Moving forward, we asked a kid named Harold Bagsby to perform with us in local talent shows. He was another excellent dancer and classmate at Wadsworth Elementary School. Still, even with Harold, our group didn't become popular until we teamed up with Devon Verse. We knew Devon was the missing link and the key to help the group be one of the more popular pop locking and breakdancing groups in the world.

We practiced after school every day for two hours for five years. A few months before we begin high school, we begin dancing together and competing against other pop locking groups. Ron Bell was the one to push me into it, but we eventually called ourselves the Star Blazers, and wore gold jackets with a four point star on the back. The group name was influenced by the Venus Electronics, which was another popular group. A member of their group dated one of Devon's sisters, and as a result the Venus Electronics began to mentor us as up-and-coming entertainers.

The more we performed, the more popular we became, and the more support we gained by older members of the community. Our name spread like fire on oil throughout Chicago, and various people, including gang members, pimps and drug dealers, began to show support in their own way. The universal support we enjoyed allowed us to travel freely and not be harassed by gang members in certain neighborhoods. It was inspiring and validated that we were doing something positive. We got so good that talent shows were paying us to perform as special guests.

I mentioned our practice dedication, and part of that stemmed from the fact that we were all perfectionists. None of us took losing well, and we enjoyed the joy we brought people. The hard work paid off in many ways, and during a practice session in the YMCA I was approached by Ms. Duckworth, a youth coordinator for the organization. She asked if we would be open to performing for one of her friends. I didn't have to think twice about agreeing. Five minutes later I danced for her friend, who at the time was an executive for Pan Am Airlines. She thoroughly enjoyed my performance and asked if we would be interested in performing for her colleagues.

Ed Sulley joined our group as the fourth member around this time. As a former gymnast and medical student, his presence helped broaden our appeal and change breakdancing forever. Through Ed's gymnastic training, we were the first to combine the windmill with the Thomas Flair. A windmill is when a breaker rolls his torso continuously in a circular path on the floor, across the upper chest/shoulders/back, while twirling his legs in a V-shape through the air. Kurt Thomas was the first American male gymnast to win a gold medal in floor exercise in a world championship. Two gymnastic moves were named for him, the Thomas Flair, a pommel horse move, and his signature on floor exercises, the Thomas salto, which was a tucked 1.5 backward salto with a 1.5 twist into a roll out (a dangerous and complex skill even by today's principles).

This combination of gymnastics and breakdancing had never been seen before. Initially, we were widely regarded as one of the top pop-locking groups. As we evolved professionally, our b-boying/breakdancing moves, Cirque du Solei approach and dramatic mix of circus arts and street entertainment helped us to gain new popularity.

After we performed for the Pan Am Airlines executives, they asked us to do an international tour. Saying that it was a huge honor is an understatement. At the time, the NYC breakers and Rock Steady Crew were the only other groups in America to perform internationally. Also, it was my coming out party as an entrepreneur. At fourteen I helped to negotiate this contract. Although we had done several shows and I negotiated the details, including compensation, travel and lodging, this was the biggest and riskiest opportunity.

On Saturday mornings during the summer, I rode my bike three miles to Jackson Park. Here I was introduced to golf and became a caddie. As a result of being a twelve-year-old caddie at a public golf course, I developed relationships with several judges, lawyers and businessmen. I watched and listened to them discuss a range of topics from court cases to million-dollar deals. My relationships and exposure yielded big dividends. I was able to get the support I needed from some of the best in the legal and business arenas. The lawyers and businessmen were so impressed with my entrepreneurial and intestinal fortitude that I became a *pro bono* case and new topic of discussion on the golf course. I even participated in the negotiation process with Pan Am from start to finish, and we landed a sponsorship deal that took us from Chicago to India. Not Indiana the state, but India the country! I was surprised that my mother let me go to New Delhi, but her words were very kind: "Although I can't help you, I'm not going to hold you back." She knew I was staying out of trouble as long as I was dancing.

We entertained hundreds of people, and the tour afforded me the opportunity to see the world through different lenses. It was like being on a goodwill tour for the U.S. The response that we got from people was incredible. On the sadder side, I was exposed to poverty at its worst while touring India. I had no idea that people lived in such harsh conditions, with so little food and shelter. Growing up on the mean streets of Chicago provided an idea of what poverty was like; however, it was nothing compared to what I saw in India and other parts of the world. The impact was so powerful that I dedicated my life to serving others. My mother and grandmother often talked about their hardships growing up in Mississippi, and they encouraged me to help people and to fight for others that were unable to defend themselves. This experience confirmed that exposure is one of the greatest gifts a person can receive. It directly combats ignorance.

As a youth, I always wondered how we were able to make such an impact on people around the world, but as I aged I understood it was because we offered hope through dance. We allowed spectators to momentarily escape from the harsh reality of life. It was an incredible feeling and a time I will never forget. I thank God for such a wonderful experience. It helped shape and mold me into the person I am today.

A high school classmate, electrifying pop locker and b-boy/break-dancer, Darryl Moore, later joined our posse. Together we became the premier group in Chicago, and one of the best in world.

Throughout my career as an entertainer, I performed hundreds of times for thousands of adoring fans. I participated in well over 300 events and plenty of talent shows, and we always won. Once I performed against R. Kelly at a Kenwood Academy high school talent show, and he and his group came in second place to my crew. But it was the fans that brought joy to my heart and inspired me to use my talent to help bring change to the world.

THREE

Killer Instinct

Unfortunately, my mother's educational experience in the South was virtually identical to what I endured in the Chicago public school system. As I advanced through elementary school, I too was unprepared and performed poorly. This was due in part to a learning disability which was recognized by Mr. Herman Pruitt, my sixth-grade teacher.

As an eleven-year-old kid with undeveloped reading, writing and analytical skills, school was very intimidating. Mr. Pruitt's approach didn't ease my anxiety in the least because he was demanding. Mr. Pruitt was kind, tough, fair and expected students to excel. Every Friday, he delegated a special assignment for homework, which required reading the newspaper and writing a one page essay about an article that was considered to be positive. Nearly every Monday before we submitted the essay, he called on students to stand up in front of the entire class and read the article aloud. Since my reading comprehension, writing and analytical skills were undeveloped, it was the most terrifying experience. Students laughed as I struggled to read and pronounce words. It was tough. Part of me wanted to scream and punch the next person that laughed. The other parts of me wanted drop everything and leave the classroom. I put forth my best effort and was rewarded with laughter. It was humiliating and killed my spirit.

To help improve my reading skills and build my confidence, Mr. Pruitt sent me to a reading specialist three days a week. To succeed, most people need someone to believe in and support their dream. The additional work helped to improve my skills and confidence tremendously, but I was still reading on a third grade level. Mr. Pruitt was an amazing teacher and I owe a lot to him. Back then, I didn't pay as much attention to the notion as I do now, but I looked up to him like a father I never knew.

When I progressed to seventh grade the following year I was no longer able to work with a reading specialist, and all the progress I made was lost along with my volition to succeed. Sometimes we don't get what we want in life, and I should have taken it upon myself to read more and study harder. As a student, I had a responsibility to give my best effort and to teach myself the curriculum. I lacked the hunger and ability to understand the value of education and how it inspired innovation, technology and ideas that have changed the world. Mr. Pruitt once said that I didn't have to be a great reader to read, but I had to get started to be great.

Today I live by the code: "don't regret what you failed to do in the past, regret what you are not doing right now." Discover your talent and develop it accordingly to make a positive impact on society and empower your community. I am confident that it will help you prosper, live your dreams and soar to new heights.

HYDE PARK HIGH SCHOOL

My first day of high school is one day I will never forget. I woke up brimming with excitement about the unknown possibilities of the day ahead. The unknown has always been quite appealing to me. I believe that when you don't know what will happen next you are given the fuel to make your dreams become a reality.

On that fateful, warm Monday morning, I jumped up and dressed myself in a plaid shirt, khaki slacks and sneakers. Although my mother suggested that I wear new clothes to school on the first day, the older kids in my neighborhood warned that wearing new clothes would ostracize me and perhaps cause bullies to gravitate toward me. Still overflowing with eagerness, I prepared an easy breakfast of pancakes, a piece of bacon, two eggs and a glass of milk. I walked to school with a few of my friends, mostly older guys, and we all dressed in older fashions to blend in. As I approached the high school I noticed other freshmen donned in new clothes. They were all running into the building to avoid being hit by

> Action may not always bring happiness; but there is no happiness without action...
>
> - Benjamin Disraeli

the crab apples being thrown by upper-class-men standing across the street in a park field. At that moment I understood the power of association and why the older guys in my neighborhood stressed the importance of wearing old clothes and being seen with older students on the first day. Being associated with older students gave me instant credibility with gang bangers, athletes, cheerleaders and the elite student body. History suggests that if I were to ever excel, I would need more allies than enemies.

Being the natural leader that I am, I began to form friendships with people throughout the school that were influential or popular. Anyone can understand that if you get the support of mighty people you can accomplish anything. People are powerful. They possess the greatest natural resource on the face of the earth: the human spirit. The spirit is a great tool. It mobilizes people to move, act, change and broaden their horizons.

High school is considered by many to be the most important time in a young person's life. Most teenagers experience things that their parents cannot prepare them for, and they give into the peer pressures that beg them to experiment with things like sex and drugs. To combat such pressure, an enormous amount of willpower must be displayed. Willpower is often described as being in control of one's impulses and actions, but it is also associated with determination and self-control. I learned first-hand that having such an attribute would help me survive past the age of sixteen.

I recall a time during my sophomore year when classes for the day adjourned and I was on my way home. As I exited I saw gang fights taking place all around the school and throughout a park that was adjacent to the building. I knew that I had to get home somehow and avoid the fights, so I ran as fast as I could toward 63rd street, where a Chicago Transit Authority (CTA) bus was parked, filled with students.

As I approached the bus I heard someone shout,

"get him." When I looked back there were several Black Gangster Disciples armed with bats sprinting toward me. I don't know if they were referring to me, but I wasn't about to slow down to find out. I ran faster toward the bus, but the closer I got, the faster the wheels rotated away from my reach. I got within five feet and it accelerated to a speed that I could not match running, but I continued chasing, knowing that if I stopped I would be in serious trouble. The bus proceeded to the next stop which was a block away. I kept up pursuit, hoping to arrive on time to be admitted.

Unfortunately, I was a few seconds too late, and it lurched forward again. This pattern recurred for four blocks, which is equivalent to a half mile. Due to my fear of failure, and an even greater desire to succeed in not being beaten to death, I finally arrived before the bus door closed and was accepted aboard for fifty cents. The driver looked at me and released a hearty laugh.

I asked why he made me chase him for four blocks, and he replied, "If I stopped and waited for you, the guys that were chasing you would have caught up and everyone on this bus would be endangered. I go through this every day when I pass by your high school. The gangs are out of control, and I am tired of being hit with flying objects or watching students being pulled through the window onto the street while we're moving. Thugs are constantly targeting me, and the city of Chicago doesn't pay enough for all that."

"I'm not in a gang," I said between breaths. "I was running 'cause they were fighting and attacking everyone in sight."

"Have a seat, kid."

"I'll stand."

"Okay," he started, releasing a hearty laugh from his belly. "You're going to do great things one day."

To my malcontent, this running-for-my-life-chasing-a-moving-bus episode went on for several months until the driver finally decided that when he saw me running for his bus, he would slow down enough to allow me to get on to prevent my getting hurt by gang members.

Over the next two years, the driver and I became good friends, and he transitioned into somewhat of a mentor to me. Having him as a mentor was great and I learned a lot about life, which helped me look at things from a different perspective. Before meeting him I walked, thought and acted like a boy. I didn't understand manhood or what it took to be a man. I was operating in a small world consisting of things that the average teenager would consider to be important. As a teenager I only thought about things that affected me.

Unlike many of my peers, I never experiment with drugs or alcohol because I saw the negative effect it had on people. However, I did experiment with sex, and like a typical teenager I was very curious about it. Similar to anyone in my position, I was reluctant to date girls at times because of all the pressure associated with it. If I could turn back the hands of time I would have waited to have sex. I learned a lot about myself as a result of the experience, but it also snatched away any remaining bits of innocence.

At the tender age of thirteen, I became a young adult in the eyes of my peers. Although I knew very little about sex, it didn't stop me from acting like I was an expert. I began having intercourse before I underwent sex education class. The closest thing to education I acquired was from my peers and several older guys that were supposed to be well-experienced.

The older guys frequently discussed sex, and like a fly on the wall I often stood a few feet away and soaked up every word. Without a father to tell me they were wrong, it was all I knew. It took me back to when I was first going through puberty and I had my first erotic dream. I didn't have anyone to talk to about the situation, but listening to them made me more comfortable with myself. I began to understand that I wasn't abnormal or weird and that the changes in my body were normal and everyone went through them. Several of these guys had girlfriends, a growing fan club and a lot of swagger. This gave them a lot of credibility, and when they discussed sex, I believed that I could achieve what they openly discussed.

Growing up in a multigenerational, woman-led household has its advantages, but the disadvantages led me to seek advice about sex and life from men that lied about the majority of their experiences. The impact an absent father can have on a boy is unquantifiable. I made several mistakes as a youth because the advice I received ensured that I was misinformed, bamboozled and led astray. To this day, I sometimes wonder how different my life would have been had I receive the mentorship and guidance from my father and not from other misinformed young men.

THE COLLEGE YEARS

My good friend Brian Woods once said, "In life, sometimes you cannot write a chapter, sometimes chapters write themselves." Following true to his words, my life as a college student wrote itself.

Like many other eighteen-year-old, African-American males from the ghettos across America, I too wanted to pursue and play professional sports with the hopes of becoming a millionaire. Outside my athletic fantasies, I was undecided about my career aspirations and what I wanted out of life. I had played sports since pampers were fashionable, and it made sense to me to become a professional athlete. Athletes are in the public's eye and admired. In my hood, it was popular to become a pimp, player, hustler, thief, gangster or thug. None of my family had attended college when I first considered the possibility. College just wasn't a conversation we held in my household or neighborhood. No discussions meant no thoughts for me.

After spending five years in high school and graduating with a D average, I had no idea where my life was headed. I stopped break dancing because I still had aspirations to become a professional baseball player, but I damaged my arm throwing curve balls and not properly training. During this period break-dancing was becoming less popular and the gang activity was continuing to spread.

One day while I was walking I stopped by the basketball court, and a gentleman by the name of Henry Ray asked me what I was doing now that I had graduated from high school. I hadn't thought much of it before, but his words caused me to realize that I was clueless as to which direction my life was heading. He suggested that I consider attending college because I could play baseball, and it would expose me to a new environment and provide me with an avenue to try something different. I trusted Henry. He lived in my community and was seen as an activist who had help hundreds of young African-American and minority students attend college and live their dreams. I decided to take him up on his offer, and he helped me get admitted into Alabama State University (a historically black university located in Montgomery, Alabama).

Like all students, I was required to take the ACT. Though I completed the examination, I received one of the lowest scores possible: 10. The lowest score possible is a 1, but that's virtually non-existent, and the 1st percentile is 1-11 (1% of ACT takers score below an 11). The highest possible score is a 36, but the 99th percentile starts at 32.

Today the national average is around 20-21.

Again, taking a standardized test was like being taught how to boil pasta in school, when the test requires Coq Au Vin, but this time around was worse. It was like trying to make Coq Au Vin without a kitchen. Halfway through the test I simply stopped. I had no clue what I was doing. To finish, I just filled in random numbers. It was one of the first times I had absolutely no idea how to solve the problem presented before me. I wouldn't say I gave up, because to give up I would have to have a chance at passing, and I simply didn't have an iota of an inkling of what the solutions to the problems were. I wasn't ashamed at my score. It accurately reflected my skill level as a student athlete during this period in my life. Despite my low ACT score, ASU helped ignite new possibilities and resources during a time when I was considering quitting.

I attended Alabama State University for a year, withdrawing both semesters to prevent a failing grade, before packing my things and heading home. I worked a bit and played some basketball before making the decision to attend Stillman College, a small liberal arts school located in Tuscaloosa, Alabama. Stillman College was a decent school, but my inadequate academic foundation came screaming back like a banshee and I failed again. I was unable to maintain a 2.0 (had a close 1.98), which was required to remain a student.

Once again I took some time off, but decided to enroll in a few summer courses at Kennedy King Community College (Chicago). I passed all of my classes with As and Bs, but needed straight As, so I still was not admitted into my second year at Stillman. It's hard to get perfect scores when you can barely read.

I was still undecided about my future and decided to dedicate years of my life to the U.S. Army as a reservist. The military is a great option for students who are unable to afford college or who are seeking to acquire a new challenge, gain discipline, jumpstart growth, or gather a non-traditional education that is transferable to any work force.

To get into the military I had to take another test. Nervous, I feared the worst, and though it was not an easy test for me, I did excel in one particular area: the general knowledge section.

After passing the test I went into basic training at Fort Leonard Wood, Missouri. It was 1990, and for the first time I was exposed to America in a different light. All sorts of diversity sprang open my eyes and mind. Anything from racial variances to all sorts of strength, I saw it all. I witnessed grown guys crying in the middle of the night because they were lonely or falling apart from the pressures of a drill instructor. I witnessed the liquid lack of determination seeping from the eyes of the men who weren't ready yet.

Basic training was tough for my peers, and there was almost always someone trying to wake up and run away because they couldn't stand the pressure of being yelled at all day. I laugh when I think about how easy it was for me to endure whatever a drill instructor had to say to me. I had a mother with a rifle that threatened to kill me once, what's a drill instructor going to do? Spit on me when he talks? Basic training was almost like an outlet. It let me escape the difficulties of life. I could just workout and listen to the instruction of another person with very little pressure on the decisions that I made.

While they were in bed crying, I was doing pushups and situps every night at 0100 to condition my body and mind. I knew they just weren't ready yet, so I almost found it funny that they were falling apart under the scrutiny of someone that had no real power or desire to inflict physical pain on them (minus a few sore muscles).

My conditioning progressed to the point that I would approach drill sergeants and ask *them* if I could do pushups instead of having them approach me. They would always say go ahead and then walk away. Sometimes, I'd stay down there and do pushups for hours, resting for breaks when I needed to, then pushing right back up until the drill sergeant returned and told me to leave. A few times they thanked me for making their day.

Keeping in line with my desire to help others, I sometimes requested to take other soldiers' pushup punishments, knowing that if I helped them out the whole group would succeed. Times like that developed my team-first mentality further, but I didn't just try to help others in ways that also benefited myself. I did whatever I could to help other people prepare for the hardships of training as well.

At first I wasn't acknowledged as a leader, but eventually my superiors talked enough about me that I was recognized. They gave me fast food as a reward (which took me back to my affection toward my grandmother when she would reward me with a cake tasting), and that was as good as gold during basic. I was the brains behind the bunch because of my gang experience and prior environment.

Tragically, there was also a bit of gang trouble within the military. Judges would often give a decision to a youth facing jail time: either prison or the military. For the ones that chose the military, every so often a rival would be in as well, but I was able to help diffuse those situations since I'd done it so many times before. There were even times when I'd persuade gang members not to commit suicide or kill the drill sergeants. I persuaded many soldiers to hang in and keep fighting until they served their term. If one person failed in the unit, everyone may.

After my military stint I decided to attend Jacksonville State University, located in Jacksonville, Alabama. Returning to civilian life was like visiting a brand new world. Despite the shock, I was able to maintain a 2.0 after two years of school. I still wasn't a stellar student thanks to my foundation, and everything was difficult. I simply was not ready and the only thing in my favor was confidence. Luckily, confidence has been one of the few things that I've always had an abundance of. Regardless of what my life suggests, I've always thought I could do anything. Back when I lived in the hood, a lack of confidence could easily mean the end of your life. Post-Jacksonville I returned to Chicago to work and complete my education at Roosevelt University and DePaul

University.

Prior to attending DePaul University, I enrolled at Roosevelt University to obtain a paralegal certificate. I thought it would be a great opportunity to learn about the law and acquire a position as a paralegal to help pay for the remainder of my education. My overall experience was splendid. The people were cordial and accommodating.

The paralegal program was strenuous though, mainly because I lacked the academic tools and endurance to succeed. The program consisted of several courses, including criminal law, real estate law and legal research. I failed every course except one. Again I endured the sting of defeat. Putting in the massive amount of effort and still not seeing the first four letters of the alphabet made me want to quit.

I needed to get away so I traveled back and forth from Chicago to Oxnard, California, to spend time with Helen Vaughn. I was dating her at the time while pursuing a modeling and acting career. I spent a lot of time in Los Angeles, and my time there was humbling. There were so many attractive and talented people. I made a little money modeling which inspired me to go on a few auditions and try to make it as an actor. Eventually I added that to my book of failures. I'd always liked the entertainment industry and figured why not give it a shot? Though I'd failed, I don't regret trying. It made me hungry and helped me to be more focused.

While in California I was reintroduced to my faith through Helen, who was very spiritual. She had a daughter, but had decided to remain celibate until marriage, and thus I was celibate for a while as well. She shared her relationship with God with me, and I enjoyed church, but Bible study was really where I loved to be. I could talk and ask questions and listen, and I gobbled up the whole situation.

For Christmas that year (1993), Helen gave me a sleek black Bible with silver writing. She left a note inside the pages, that's still there, conveying that she hopes the book blesses me as much as it blessed her. It's the only Bible I've ever owned, and I've held onto it for years.

Reading it changed my life, and I flipped through the entire thing. I started praying and developing my vocabulary. Whenever I encountered a word I didn't understand, I looked it up and wrote it down. Reading the book also helped boost my comprehension, propelling me from a fifth to a seventh-grade reading level. I was able to interpret information better, my stamina for reading increased and it revitalized a hunger for knowledge in me. Reading and being able to read better gave me something to talk about, unleashing a special part of me.

I returned to Chicago with a new attitude and re-enrolled into the program. This go around I completed every course with a passing grade or honors. Reading through the Bible allowed me to get a lot more out of books, and eventually I started reading through the dictionary, as well. I also read the Autobiography of Malcolm X (By Alex Haley) around that time, which inspired me to read through the dictionary the way he did. I started at the letter *A*, learning to write out every word and definition. I even used them all in a sentence. Knowing so many more words helped me storm through any school-related readings I had.

Finishing up the paralegal program was a great stepping-stone for me, and I soon enrolled into DePaul University to complete my undergraduate studies in liberal arts, political science and philosophy. Reading through the Bible also helped me understand the philosophy textbooks and Shakespeare, among countless other works of literature. The gap was still present, and I still struggled, but I managed to achieve all A's and B's at DePaul.

I started seeing Renee Salahudine, who was twelve years my elder and an educator. Knowing my inadequate educational foundation, she took on the role of a tutor, helping me write and edit papers.

I don't think my decision to date someone else was conscious, but as my skills developed, I also started seeing Lena Casimir. She was a college graduate and nerd who loved biology (she eventually became a dentist). Renee continued to tutor me even when we stopped dating, and I owe her a great deal for that. I'm convinced she is one of the most gifted educators I've ever encountered. She understood where I came from and what I lacked, and her patience with me was phenomenal. Working with her further compounded my educational confidence, and I felt I could conquer the world.

Lena was also instrumental in my education. She was a lovely and kind person who tutored me as well (I'm starting to realize a pattern with the people I dated), but she made me embarrassed over how little I knew. At one point she assumed I should know what a run-on sentence was despite my ignorance of the concept. I was hurt by how she failed to recognize how little I actually comprehended about grammar. She was also the victim of a bad school system, but her life had been the exception while mine had been the rule. Just like Renee, Lena was a catalyst in aiding the improvement of my academic performance and study habits. They were both gigantic inspirations to me.

During the process of completing my course work at DePaul University in the evening, I worked Monday through Friday, nine A.M. to five P.M., as a law clerk at the City of Chicago Department of Revenue. It was an intense period. DePaul University's academic calendar was offered on a quarter system that allowed students to take classes all year long. Typically, I took a full course load each quarter, and whenever I could I would add two additional classes, giving me a total of twenty-one credits for the quarter. I even took courses on weekends at other institutions of higher learning. I was so hungry and determined to finish my undergraduate studies that I typically slept five hours, worked eight hours, traveled three hours on the train and bus and studied eight hours a day. I usually threw in an exercise regimen as well. Staying physically fit is important to every other aspect of life. I was willing to die before I failed, and a voracious tenacity to succeed erupted from every pore in my body.

My mother's communication with me still wasn't the greatest, and while at home one day she uttered a statement that cut me deeply: "I don't know why in the hell you're going to school. You're wasting your time. You might as well save your money."

I didn't know what else to do or how to reply aside from slapping a smile on my face and saying, "I'm going to school because it is what I am supposed to be doing. It's the only way." Though she was still emotionally damaging, she continued to motivate me.

To further fuel my hunger, my English professor asked me to come by his office one day to discuss a paper I had submitted. During our conversation, he stated that my writing skills were horrible before questioning me about my career aspirations. I replied with my desire to become a lawyer one day and somehow help change the world.

He bluntly said that trying to become a lawyer was unrealistic thinking on my behalf and that, and I quote, "You people are good with your hands, so you should consider doing something with your hands like welding or carpentry."

I look back on the situation and gawk at how similar my experience in this matter was to Malcolm X's experience, though our reactions differed greatly. On a side note, my professor was unaware that I frequently attended court and watched lawyers argue during my lunch hour because I wanted to become an attorney. I studied their body language, attention to detail, professional attire, eye contact, communication skills and how they went about building relationships. I was committed to fulfilling my dream and gaining the necessary exposure to ensure my success. To say I was shocked and bewildered that he would make such a statement doesn't really convey the meaning accurately, but it's as close as I can come to my reaction.

My first instinct was to assault him for his statements, but instead, while trying to keep composure, I replied by thanking him for his kindness. It took a mustering of every ounce of strength that I had gathered from the aggregate experiences in my past to give him a civilized response, but inside I was fuming.

I went on to say, "Although I recognize that you are an educator, I'm paying a lot of money to go to this school, and I thought your job as an educator was to inspire me, to mold me and to shape me as a person and as a student. If you look at a lot of the students here, everyone is sitting in class and they are at different academic levels. As an educator, I know you recognize that, and part of your job is to look at where we are and get us to a certain level. In areas where I'm deficient, your job is to make me efficient.

But instead, you chose to tell me what I am not going to be or what I shouldn't try to accomplish. And because I lack the certain academic skills today, doesn't mean I won't acquire those skills to better myself. Your job is to ensure that I get those skills, so I can, if I choose, become a lawyer. Or create a successful career for myself. How could you void your responsibility, your fiduciary duties to lead, teach and inspire? You aren't doing what you get paid to do."

My professor was a Caucasian, middle-aged male who had many preconceived notions about African Americans. Subsequently, I had a long conversation with the dean of the English department,

> **To be American is to be epic...**
>
> **- Ron Mitchell**

my academic advisor Pat Ryan and the president of the university. We discussed the conversation I had with my English professor, and I shared with them all my frustration and disappointment. Pat insisted that I converse with the president, and I did speak with Rev. John P. Minogue, CM. During this period he was the president of DePaul University, and as expected he was very kind throughout our conversation, applauding my bravery and assuring me that the travesty would never happen again. The experience made me even hungrier and provided me with the blind motivation that I needed during such a challenging period of time.

A lot of students would have given up, but I didn't. Miss Toby Glicken, another educator, helped progress my studies in science. Miss Glicken had a background in logic and reasoning, even though I took science-based courses from her. After I told her I was interested in becoming a lawyer she helped me overcome my fears and improve in the areas I needed to improve. She helped me tackle math and logical reasoning without fear, and she inspired me to write and read even more.

Science and math were my Achilles tendon, but through her ability to work and talk with me, I received the courage necessary to not only dream big, but to hope while pursuing my dreams. I always had confidence, but she infused my confidence with hope. I had fallen away from my drive to change the world, but she kindled the flames of change within my heart until they burned brighter than ever. Sometimes, you have to take a negative situation and use it as fuel to help achieve your goals. To overcome adversity and gain the winning edge, you will need to make the impossible possible.

Law school - LSAT attempts and how I made it through

Many kids grow up dreaming about becoming a lawyer, but I never even imagined attending law school, yet alone graduating. As a result of my background and lack of exposure, I didn't know what a lawyer was or did until I entered college.

Growing up in a drug and gang-infested ghetto, and attending a Chicago public school, which was viewed by many as among the worst in the country, I was not exposed to certain professions outside of your typical police officer and fire fighter. My mother and teachers never talked about career options. They didn't really encourage me or most of my peers to consider a profession based upon our passions and talents. Becoming a doctor or lawyer was a conversation reserved for the majority of the Jewish teammates on my summer league baseball team. I always wondered why they were talking about law and medicine. It was boring to me and made little to no sense. My personal experiences have confirmed that we become and or believe whatever we digest. Diversity of thought is imperative for success. It fuels imagination and hope, inspiring new possibilities.

When I was in college I was granted the opportunity

to participate in the John Marshall School of Law pre-law summer institute. It was a summer program designed to expose college students to law school and provide a foundation for the future. I enjoyed this program because it did provide me with greater insight than I had prior to participating in the program.

After graduating from college, I was excited about attending law school largely in part to the programs that supported and inspired me to seek a legal career. On the cusp of entering, my grandmother took sick and eventually died. On her journey to the end she was suffering from the later

> The super man is in us, only if we learn to discover it...
>
> - Akinyande Ayomide

stages of Alzheimer's but remained at home. Before she passed I was away working as a law clerk at the Department of Revenue, but my instincts told me to go home and be with my family. I ignored the feeling and tragedy struck. My brother was at home with her, watching television and smoking a cigarette when he fell asleep. The smouldering stick slipped from his fingers and found kindling on the sofa, where it erupted into a fire. My grandmother was rescued from the fire, but the soot inhaled into her lungs created pneumonia. She died a few weeks later. I blamed myself for not being there to help take care of her, and I carried that burden with me into law school, learning an invaluable lesson from the situation: always trust your instincts.

I never imagined how tough it was to get admitted into a law school. Although I had faced many obstacles in my life, this was the most time consuming and challenging. It was the most intellectually taxing road, and I felt alone. I was traversing a trail none of my peers ever even considered.

Like most students, I enrolled in a LSAT preparation course in order to be admitted into a good law school. My experience with the course I took was rotten because it didn't prepare me for the examination. The first course was poorly taught, most likely attributed to the fact that the instructor had taken the LSAT and mastered the testing process. This sounds good, but mastering a test and teaching others how to do the same are not equal skills.

Because of the rotten quality of my first attempt, I took another LSAT course from a different well-respect organization. Unfortunately, it was very similar to the first preparation course, and the strategy taught was not tailored to different learning styles because the instructor didn't excel at the most important skill: teaching. The best instructors are able teach, simplify information and address any questions asked.

Despite my poor experience with two of America's leading LSAT preparatory courses (one of them being the Princeton Review) I pushed forward, studied hard and took the exam. I tried my best, but did very poorly, yet I wasn't deterred. I was more motivated than ever because I knew that I could improve my scores. I studied for months and took every old examination that I could get my hands on to prepare for my retake. I did make a nice improvement the second time around, but it wasn't good enough to admit me into my school of choice. Feeling defeated after giving your best is the worst experience in the world.

During my studies for the LSAT, I ran into a gentleman (I can't remember his name for the life of me, so I will refer to him as Josh) who introduced me to a paralegal program at his place of employment: Kirkland and Ellis. I worked with Kirkland and Ellis for a year while studying and waiting to attend law school, and I learned a great deal. Since it was a large law firm I exposed myself to a place where many prestigious lawyers worked.

Kirkland and Ellis was put on the largest litigation

cases (one case related to when the tobacco industry was getting sued. Kirkland and Elis was hired as counsel to represent Brown & Williamson, which was a large tobacco company). One thing that I noticed, though I'm ashamed to say I didn't think was odd, was that 98-99 percent of the attorneys were white.

While at the firm I worked with a number of attorneys, many who admired my work ethic. They liked me because of my hard work (which, by the way, is one of the most important factors in becoming successful), though I'm sure many also enjoyed my company because they did not view me as a threat. I also observed that almost all the attorneys acted the same, digested the same intellectual material, ate the same and even physically resembled one another. Everything was uniform and ritualistic. Of all the things I took away from that experience, the salient one is the encouragement that I received from them to pursue my dreams as a lawyer. They verbalized how sharp I was, and this swept away any doubt I harbored toward taking the bar one day.

All in all, I devoted an entire year to the LSAT. I really wanted to attend law school and make a difference like the late Thurgood Marshall, a man whom I admired and drew strength from throughout my journey.

While overwhelmed with my studies, I faced a crossroad. I lacked the emotional energy to continue, but my friend Josh's words gave me the boost I needed: "If you really want to do something you will find a way. If you don't, you'll find an excuse."

I went online to find the help that I needed to gain an edge and improve my chances of being admitted. Ms. Loretta Deloggio's name came up through a search I did for LSAT preparatory courses. I decide to devote another six months to the LSAT and begin working with Lorretta. Her classes were taught in different locations across America, and I had to fly to Alexandria, Virginia, to participate in her course.

It was an awesome experience and she helped me understand why I previously hadn't performed well. Through her, I was able to digest how I lacked the foundation and confidence in my intellectual ability. She also videotaped me sometimes during my practice exams to help me see how I looked. We even went over breathing techniques to help quell my nervousness-induced hyperventilation.

I learned how to trust myself academically and to believe in a process. Historically, and throughout my academic career, I had always performed poorly on standardized tests. I often changed my answers during the examination because I didn't trust my instincts. This type of behaviour caused me to receive low scores. Her methods installed a strategy into my test taking, and a new confidence emerged. I took my gusto from athletics and the streets and transformed it into classroom confidence, eventually taking the LSAT a third time and making a noticeable improvement, allowing me to become more competitive. Loretta also pointed out most LSAT retake scores don't improve more than a single point, or they decrease, but mine had undergone a drastic change in a positive direction.

To further prepare myself for law school, and to improve my chances of gaining admission, I applied to the Council on Legal Education Opportunity (CLEO) Program. CLEO was founded in 1968 as a non-profit project of the ABA Fund for Justice and Education to expand opportunities for minority and low-income students to attend law school. Congress passed the Higher Education Amendments Act in 1998, which established the Thurgood Marshall Legal Educational Opportunity Program. CLEO was subsequently selected to administer the program.

The mission of the CLEO program is to help

expand legal education opportunities to minority, low-income and disadvantaged groups. Today, more than 8,000 students have participated in CLEO's pre-law and law school academic support programs, successfully matriculated through law school, passed the bar exam and joined the legal profession. CLEO alumni consist of several professionals that had less than traditional academic indicators of success, yet were given an opportunity to attend law school. As a result, many are represented in every area of society, including corporations and private law firms, law schools, federal and state judiciaries and legislatures across America.

Annually, the CLEO program receives hundreds of applications. Selected students are required to take part in a six-week residential program designed to prepare participants to be more competitive students. During the residential program, law professors representing many of the best law schools in the nation teach law school courses. Those who successfully complete the program become CLEO fellows and were eligible for scholarships during law school.

When I participated in the program, many of the other students had already gained admission into law schools like Harvard, Yale, Michigan and Georgetown

University. CLEO is well-respected and representatives from many of the top law schools visited the program to recruit students that had not been admitted. Law schools are always trying to funnel the best and brightest in the world to their campuses.

Academically, I did well and completed the program. As a result, several programs attempted to recruit me. I was offered a scholarship and decided to attend the University of Pittsburgh. Although it was an eighteen-month process to gain admission into law school, it was worth the wait. I learned that being patient is truly a virtue.

The easiest thing to do in life is to quit and give up on your dreams or goals. To succeed, you must be willing to do the things that most people will not do today in order to have the success that others will not experience tomorrow.

LAW SCHOOL EXPERIENCE

My law school expedition was a life-changing experience. I learned a lot about myself and was challenged in ways that I never imagined. Law school is a breeding ground for some of the most brilliant minds across the globe. It has produced presidents, politicians, leaders and a long list of individuals that have made great contributions to the world. I am grateful to have experienced what few people have, which is to spar intellectually with some of the best and brightest minds, to be challenged emotionally, mentally and physically in an academic environment.

During orientation week I attended a mandatory seminar for drug abuse. It was a good seminar and made me aware of the heavy drug abuse in the legal community. As a result of the pressure to perform well academically, many students often turn to drugs to cope emotionally, mentally and psychologically. I have never used drugs, but my upbringing was riddled with eye-witness accounts of the negative impact they can have on a human being. Thankfully, I never witnessed another student use drugs in law school because the people I associated with didn't use.

The pressure to do well in law school is epic due to the relentless and raw nature of the studies. Some of the brightest people flunk out because they are unable to deal with the pressure for various reasons. For some, it is a lack of support from their family and friends.

During my first week I often heard professors say, "Look to your left and look to your right." After pausing for effect, they would add: "One of them will not be around in three years." They were right, and some of my classmates dropped out after the first year, and some during the second year, for different reasons.

Although I loved the intellectual challenge, my excursion was made more arduous because I was one of two African Americans in my section at school. In the fall of 1999, I experienced a lot of racism and became the target of a lot of racist comments. I was called several names including nigger, but the most memorable of them all was "Mr. Affirmative Action."

Approximately 300 students were divided into three sections my first year. In the fall of 1999, approximately eleven African Americans were admitted (seven males and six females, which at the time was a very large class for the University of Pittsburgh School of Law).

I was put in a section with Yolanda Trotman, a kind and brilliant person. We were the only non-white students in the section out of 100. Our unique experiences in life and law school enabled us to develop a bond that I still cherish. Unfortunately, we did not study together, although we were in the same section.

In law school there is an enormous amount of pressure to write a lot and to read even more. It is considered by most to be a very conservative and cutthroat environment. This environment prompts professors to suggest that students develop study groups to help deal with the pressure and to better comprehend the massive amount of material assigned.

During my first year I often studied by myself because other students did not want to study with me, which made things tough. Paradoxically, I felt isolated in the crowd of my peers, like a black pit bull surrounded by greyhounds. I heard many of my white peers complain about how horrible the environment was every day, but for me it was twice as hard. I was forced to overcome a learning disability, study alone, ignore racist comments targeted at me and then endure the same academic pressure they did. To put things mildly, my relationships with some professors were very interesting.

Typically, after I sat through a lecture for one and a half hours, I waited patiently along with other students to speak with the professor to confirm that I understood different concepts. Whenever I asked a question, my professors would be kind and give me an answer, but their responses were brief and at times ambiguous. It was difficult to gain a sound understanding of the specific legal concepts. Whenever other white students asked questions, the professors were aptly accommodating. They would go the extra miles to ensure the concepts were understood. Simply put, I was treated different and it affected my confidence and ability to learn.

I was hungry and had to find a way to get my questions answered to ensure that I did well on my final examinations. I developed a strategy of asking a few students in each of my classes to ask questions on my behalf at the end of each lecture. While they asked questions, I would stand a few feet behind them, listening closely and taking notes.

Initially the people I solicited for help assumed I was joking, but after a few examples and trials they saw that I was serious and continued to assist. The strategy worked and changed the game by helping to build my confidence and improve my grades.

In the military I was taught how to improvise, and this was a situation where my training came in handy. Faced with adversity, I was able to implement an unconventional approach to achieve my goal. Still, since every professor knew who I was, I find it hard to believe that they graded me anonymously, which raises the question of how fair my grades were. There were also a few situations where I managed to get an unfair grade changed to a more appropriate one, and one time sticks out in my mind. I wrote an essay that yielded a *C* on an exam, but the argument made by the professor did not make sense to

> **You don't need to reinvent the wheel; you need to make it spin...**
>
> - Ikhwan Sopa

me. I checked the material and my argument, but did not see the same flaw the professor claimed I had presented.

A little unsure with how right I was, I decided to ask a peer to analyze their essay. After reviewing it I noticed we had the same argument, but they had received an *A*. The only differences in our essays were on the surface. A few words different here or there, maybe a varied order of sentences, but overall the exact same argument and points being made.

With my peer's permission, I took their exam and my exam to the professor, demanding how I received a lower grade than my peer when our essays were virtually the same. The teacher crumbled and changed the grade, which was rare, but I still wonder how many other grades I received that should have been higher?

My favorite and toughest course during my first

year of law school was legal writing. Mr. Kevin Deasey was my writing instructor. Being kind and an excellent lecturer didn't stop most students from despising this course because they were taught to write a different way.

Once, after submitting an assignment, I was asked to meet with professor Deasey to discuss my work. After reviewing my legal brief he suggested that I go see a psychologist. He thought I might have a learning disability. Throughout my life, I have had issues with learning (I mentioned this earlier in the book), which were first noticed by Mr. Pruitt. Despite this disability I have always toiled to succeed, but I never knew why it was so impossible to consistently learn and retain information. Professor Deasey also asked if anyone was helping me to write my briefs and memorandums because the assignments I turned in were so inconsistent. He said one moment my work looked like a promising legal scholar, and the next it appeared as though I had never stepped foot in a law school classroom. When he asked about my grades, I told him I was displeased with them and that I knew the material.

To my surprise, he informed me he had spoken to a few of my professors and that they had nothing but great things to say about my character and work ethic. He believed that my legal briefs reflected my grades after one semester of law school.

At the end of our chat he gave me some information and I made an appointment with Francis B. Colavita, Ph.D., and John R. Erbel, both who are well-respected psychologists in Pittsburgh. I took a neuropsychological evaluation and a number of recommendations were made to explain many of the problems I endured for years. They suggested that I get remedial tutoring for arithmetic because my quantitative reasoning skills were at the sixth-grade level. Also, my reading and spelling were at an eighth-grade level.

My recommendation included the following information: "Ron, should consider spending time with a learning skills specialist. Consider tape recording lecture material so that he can review the material as many times as necessary to obtain mastery. Ron's mild impairment in his basic problem tackling and solving skills, his severe impairment in generalizing a learned principle, his mildly impaired incidental memory, and his periodic lapses in vigilance appear to be due at least in part to organic factors that are beyond his control. Thus, it would be appropriate for Ron to receive the accommodation of extended time to take timed examinations. As he is approximately 100% below expectancy in these dimensions, it would be appropriate for him to receive 100% extended time for timed examinations."

Seeing the two psychologists answered many of the questions that I had compacted over the years. I have always had to work and study twice as hard as my peers throughout my life. While in law school, everyone studied long hours, but I studied for days without sleep because I was hungry to succeed. In spite of my laundry list of adversity, I was motivated to excel and live my dream, which was to graduate from law school no matter what odds were stacked against me.

The University of Pittsburgh School of Law received my evaluation and was accommodating. I got the support that I needed which helped me to succeed in law school. I owe a great debt to Ryan Sedlak, Sam Rainey and Nicole Williams. They became my study partners during my second and third year.

I also received enormous amounts of support from Arthur Ford, Shawn Buckner, Roderic Williams, Joy Smith and my law school mentor Earon Williams. Earon worked with me for many long hours to ensure that I learned concepts and excelled throughout law school. He helped me to develop a road map and overcome several obstacles throughout my journey. I am grateful for his guidance, leadership and unwavering support. He was inspiring, wise and brilliant beyond his years.

Additionally, there are no words to describe the impact Professor Darryl Jones had on my law school career. He was a catalyst for change, a tax law expert and a phenomenal lecturer. I took three courses from him (Business Organization, Federal Taxation and Corporate Taxation) during my second and third year of law school. He was also inspiring and taught me a great deal about corporate America and fuelled my business acumen. I thank God for my law school experience because I became more resilient.

At age thirty I was properly diagnosed for the first time in my life, and I attained the answers to the issues that had haunted me for years. I asked God for help, believing that He would answer my prayers, and I finally received solutions.

After graduating from law school with decent grades, I took the bar but failed by a few points. I haven't retaken it yet, but I plan to soon.

Shortly after that, I met with one of my favorite instructors, Tom Thompson. He was an adjunct professor at the University of Pittsburgh School of Law. Tom is also a corporate attorney and partner at Buchanan Ingersoll & Rooney. He taught me corporate mergers and acquisition, and I also learned a ton about complex deals, contracts and negotiations. I was able to work on several great deals, which helped me to identify my talent. Tom challenged me

> The impossible is possible. If you believe this, you can achieve anything...
>
> — Ron Mitchell

and other classmates to be thought leaders, social engineers and advocates against social injustice in and outside of the corporate arena.

A few weeks after graduation I had lunch with Tom to talk about my career. I expressed my interest in becoming a good lawyer and making an unmatched contribution to society. I shared with Tom my love for mankind, serving the American people, philanthropy, entrepreneurship and my plan to start my own company and attend business school. He asked me what business school I planned to attend, and I said I was considering Dartmouth University, Emory University and Clark Atlanta University. He stated that he thought it would be a great idea since I possessed the intellectual capital, creativity, hunger and leadership skills to be successful. He encouraged me to attend business school because I excelled in his course.

Tom believed I resembled a dear friend of his named Reginald Lewis, who he met while attending Harvard University School of Law. Reginald Lewis was a successful African-American entrepreneur and lawyer. I was honoured to be compared to such a brilliant, visionary man.

Today Tom is widely recognized as one of the best lawyers in America. We decided that working for a big law firm was not the best route to take considering my interests and raw talent. I decided to return to Chicago to volunteer at a small law firm and pursue business school. It was one of the most important decisions that I ever made, and it changed my life forever.

Business school –

A new approach to problem solving, teamwork, leadership

Attending law school was an unforgettable experience. It helped me to grow as a professional and discover my passion for business, becoming the perfect vehicle and introduction to business school.

After speaking with recruiters at a few areas of learning, I decided to attend Clark Atlanta University because it was a small school,

> A business mind is a beautiful mind...
>
> - Tom Thompson

and, according to U.S. News and World Report, it was the best return on investment.

Michael Hall, a former corporate executive and a successful entrepreneur, was the dean of admission at the time I attended Clark Atlanta University Business School. He played a major role in my success as a business student and entrepreneur. Michael was persuasive and one of the reasons I selected CAU. His vision for me included becoming the graduate student government association president, an adjunct professor, and a member of the CAU board of trustees while I was acquiring my business degree. He also said I could participate in a joint program that would allow me to take courses simultaneously at Clark Atlanta University Business School and Emory University's Goizueta Business School.

Michael believed that if I took risks and started a

company, one day I would change the world by being a giant in the business community. I received a scholarship by taking a risk and following the path he eloquently articulated to me during our meeting.

Despite this wonderful opportunity, internally I was reluctant to pursue a business degree because I didn't have a lot of exposure to quantitative courses in college. Historically, I had never done well in math or science, so I didn't know what to expect, but I was hungry and excited about working hard to achieve my goal.

Atlanta was a mixing bowl of possibilities and new opportunities, so many entrepreneurs had moved to this region of the country to introduce new business ideas to the world. It was a breath of fresh air and a new environment unlike the surroundings that I had grown accustomed to over the last three years.

In business school I learned: the greater the risk the greater the return. Also, my experiences in this environment taught me that things don't always turn out the way we hope or envision. Regardless of the long hours of concise planning, support, knowledge, money and experience, failure is always at our fingertips. The mistakes we make will allow us to grow and prosper.

My business school experience was challenging, and unlike law school, the focus was working on projects, reading business case studies, identifying issues, presenting solutions and working in in teams with other classmates. A lot of the work consisted of qualitative and quantitative analysis.

Most of my professors were well-versed in the information and possessed an enormous amount of real-world experience, which made the lectures and discussion interesting. Many of my classmates possessed years of practice in different industries, which

> If you make a mistake don't let it define you. It's what you learn from the experience that will reveal who you are as a person...
>
> - Ron Mitchell

elevated the expectations and created a cordial but competitive atmosphere.

The most memorable experience was meeting entrepreneurs from different parts of the country. They would visit the school and discuss their products and practices. As students, we dissected their business case, provided solutions to address the problems and made recommendations to ensure future success.

This experience inspired me to start GAM

Enterprise LLC, a consulting firm with a mission to help transform distressed small businesses. I started the Enterprise while I was still engulfed in my studies, and, unfortunately, it was not profitable. It was too challenging to attend classes, participate in meetings, support business development and recruit classmates and professors. As a result, the firm quickly dissolved, but it was a magnificent learning experience. It was the first company I started, and I made a lot of poor business decision and the organization suffered as a result.

Like so many other entrepreneurs, this experience didn't deter me from my desire to help people live their dreams and soar to new heights. I was encouraged and not discouraged, learning that honesty and failure is part of the process to success.

I recognized that communication is a key ingredient for relationship building. Although I had acquired a great team of talented professionals, I didn't have the relationships needed to successfully build a solid book of business. It was imperative that I was honest with myself and realize that it will take more than a great product or money to entice businesses to trust me with their future.

My mother believed that whatever happened on any

particular day would give birth to a better tomorrow if we

> **Underneath the lie is a truth that would do anything to be realized...**
> **- Mischa Toland**

embraced the positive energy throughout the universe. I began to embrace her philosophy and change my attitude. This gave me comfort and fed the frustration created by ambition and my willingness to succeed. It also pushed me to do what I had already done throughout my career, which was community service. Giving my time, money and heart to help others is something my mother instilled in me as a young boy. I have always loved bringing joy to others and making a difference in their life, but I never knew that it would provide me with a solution to my problem.

As a result of my community-service efforts with kids in urban and suburban areas, I was able to meet people from different walks of life with similar interests. Our common interests allowed me to discuss other issues like business, life and family while discovering a new world.

Although my focus was giving back to those in need, I was getting schooled first hand on how business is done. It was amazing. School never taught that commonality was the cure for causes. In other words, people typically come together for a cause (like a charitable event, sports, birthdays or school) because it is one thing they have in common.

I met several volunteers that owned small businesses, and I started offering my services. My approach was different this time around and I didn't accept any compensation. I worked as a volunteer because I sincerely wanted to help. As a volunteer I had no problem developing business because I had established relationships that were not money-driven. They were community-focused with genuine people that I liked and enjoyed being around. It was the best of both worlds. I was able to reach and inspire people, problem solve, help distressed businesses and work with young kids to help transform the community. I learned that true success is when you can share with others and make a positive impact.

Working closely with businesses and the community gave me some invaluable exposure and insight, which allowed me to analyze and identify issues. Just like people, organizations and communities have problems, I did too, and this notion compelled me to one day develop a way to improve communities. I recognized that several programs were in place, but most were either underfunded or provided the wrong type of service to address the issues. Many of America's poor communities have similar issues, despite race and culture.

For years I collected data and combed the country, traveling abroad as well to seek solutions to combat the problems that plague our communities. I interviewed parents, community leaders, educators, athletes, students, ex-convicts and successful individuals from various disciplines. This relentless investigation revealed some of the key ingredients needed to combat mediocrity and bring about change. I was hungry and determined to find a solution, eventually creating the BEM Methodology.

I accepted a position with Booz Allen Hamilton in the Washington D.C. metro area. Booz Allen Hamilton is a leading provider of management and technology consulting services to government agencies, corporations, institutions and non-profit organizations throughout the world. During my tenure there, I supported government and commercial organizations and provided change management capabilities to help transform their environment. It was a building block for my career and the beginning of a new chapter in my life.

FOUR

Make the Unimaginable a Reality

During my last semester in business school, I was sitting down talking to a classmate when I was asked to speak with kids at a local middle school in a drug-infested urban area about different careers options. I agreed to do so, but only if I could perform a mock trial about drug use and driving while intoxicated. I'm convinced that exposure is an essential ingredient for children to become successful. The school agreed with my request and I reached out to a few friends until I put together a team of skilled, young lawyers.

A case was produced and submitted to the teacher, and a few students were selected to participate. To make things a little more interesting, we had an all-female team compete against an all-male team. We had a lot of fun and the mock trial was a success. My experience with those children was gratifying. They were multitalented and represented an underserved community. After the mock trail I sat down to calculate the score and determine the victor.

While I was mulling over the winner, a student introduced herself and offered me a bottle of water because I was coughing. I thanked her and accepted the gift to quench my thirst. She thanked me for coming to her class before expressing her interest in becoming a doctor.

"What type of doctor do you want to be?" I asked, fingering the label on the water, which had become loose from condensation.

"An eye doctor," She responded, glancing away as if embarrassed.

"Why an eye doctor?"

"My grandmother is diabetic and losing her sight. I want to help save her life and other people who suffer from the same thing."

According to medical experts, having diabetes means that your body cannot control the level of sugar in your blood. If your blood sugar is too high, it can cause complications to the blood vessels in the retina. Spikes in blood sugar can sometimes cause temporary changes in

> Destiny is not a matter of chance; it is a matter of choice. It is not a thing to be waited for; it is a thing to be achieved...
>
> - William Jennings Bryan

vision, such as blurriness, that usually go away once you get your blood sugar levels back to normal. High blood sugar levels over time can lead to diabetic eye disease, which can lead to vision loss if left untreated. I was moved by what I had heard and knew that I had to develop something that could inspire children to live their dream and use their talent to help change the world.

I have experienced a lot professionally, and community service has always been the one common denominator. As a child I had always retained a desire to change the world, community by community. Part of my vision is to live for the moments I can't put into words. As a result, I was compelled to do something and subsequently founded the BEM Foundation, which stands for "Believe Every Moment Counts." Our mission is to help at-risk kids (ages 13-19) from all ethnicities and socioeconomic backgrounds. Since its inception, our programs have helped thousands of kids across the country.

I developed the BEM Methodology to combat the problems that are causing our communities to erode. This approach consists of three narrowly-tailored programs designed to help transform communities across America. Our Youth Town Halls, Power Texting Mentor Network and the Career Shadowing program have all been created to address issues where the needs are greatest. As a result of our impact we have attracted the attention of several Fortune 500 companies who have joined us in supporting our vision and

> Even when you fail, make a successful failure out of it so that in future if you happen to look at your past, you know what to do...
> - Daideepya Bhosale

efforts. Our corporate partners include General Motors, Capital One Bank, Best Buy, Time Warner, Comcast, Cox, Marriott and others.

Technology and our youth inspired me. They both consistently evolve and have a direct impact on our society. The BEM Methodology is a holistic approach to problem solving and transforming communities through these two mediums. This system helps improve our world, fuel intellectual capital and inspire youth to develop their gifts and talents.

Our methodology consists of our core principles: "Listen, Learn, Be Inspired." The BEM Methodology is a 360-degree approach that analyzes the local and global community from every angle to determine how best to deliver change. I am passionate about the work we are doing with the foundation. Hundreds of volunteers support our programs and partner with a dynamic team of professionals that personify excellence and hard work. Welton Barnes, our executive director, and Ryan Prucker, the communications director, both have helped me shape and lead this organization.

Along with my board members, Welton and Ryan have been my trusted advisors and a part of my think tank throughout this journey. Their intellectual capital, business acumen and problem-solving abilities have inspired me in ways that words cannot describe. There were many moments when I felt my vision died, but they refused to allow me to quit. I admire and love them both. They have been the wind behind my wings.

The BEM philosophy, "Listen, Learn, Be Inspired," embodied the spirit that fuels my vision. Listen: Our "Youth Town Hall" discussions are designed to provide young people with a platform opportunity to talk about actual, heartfelt subjects that are important to them. For example, we discuss peer pressure and bullying to help youth make wise decisions and avoid drug usage and gang activities. We discuss financial literacy to ensure kids understand the value of money and savings along with providing tips about how they can better finance college. We discuss health and wellness to convey the importance of maintaining a healthy diet.

In addition to tips on physical health and wellness, we also provide resources to combat depression. We discuss responsible technology use in order to combat cyber bullying and the increasing number of teen suicide as a result of Facebook and other social media. We discuss community development to convey the importance of service and the impact made when we work together.

Our town hall events connect youth with local business and community leaders to help inspire change, leadership and solutions to the problems existing in their neighborhoods. We have visited several cities across America, and during our youth town hall we work with professionals, as well as local and national leaders to serve thousands of youth.

Learn: Our "Power Texting Mentor Network" uses mobile technology to provide students with common sense, life-coaching skills and decision-making strategies to combat bullying and peer pressure. Professionals from all walks of life provide mentorship through cell phone texts to remind youth of things like the importance in maintaining a healthy lifestyle and diet, the value in increasing financial literacy and understanding, and the life-saving power of avoiding drunk driving and texting while driving.

Youth are paired up with professionals who act as Power Text Mentors in their area of interest. For example: if a student is interested in becoming a lawyer, he/she will be mentored by an attorney. The attorney mentor provides inspiration and a *roadmap* to encourage and guide them through high school so that one day they can become a successful lawyer. Studies show that youth are more inclined to listen to someone they admire and who is currently doing what they aspire to become one day. Our Power Text Mentors are assigned to a youth and are required, on a daily basis, to go online and log onto our automated system and review information about the youth, which is presented by the young person's parents. This information outlines what the student is having difficulty with in school, peers, etc. Next, to help combat the problems the Power Texting Mentor will send a tailored text message based on the issues the youth is currently facing. The text messages encourage sound decision making, promoting a change in behavior. Our Power Texting Mentors are assigned to a youth for a six-month period.

I created this program because the average teenager sends more than six text messages every hour (according to Nielsen, which analyzed mobile phone usage of 13 to 17 year olds). Additionally, an average teenager sends or receives 3,339 texts a month, which is a 443% rise in the second quarter in monthly data used by teenagers from a year ago. If we are going to change behavior we must meet youth where they are, and texting is now one of the most popular way to communicate among youth.

This program will be offered in several languages to serve youth and communities around the world, inspiring change. The Power Texting Mentor Network program was promoted in Best Buy stores. A link to the commercial which was seen in stores can be found at the end of the book in the resources section.

Be Inspired: Our Career Shadowing Program called "Make the Unimaginable a Reality," pairs mentors with youth that have an interest in their areas of expertise. This program was designed to expose youth to various careers and fuel inspiration for college. Here, youth are also provided with face-to-face interaction. The youth will spend an entire day with the professional, working alongside them to gain real-life experience and a better understanding about their career interest. They also learn about hard work, sacrifice and how to achieve their goals. I developed this program because, as mentioned before, I believe exposure is a key component to achieving your dreams.

Continuous Refinement & Development: the BEM Foundation is constantly working to meet the ever-changing needs of our youth, adapt to advancements, create novel outreach mediums and forge new relationships. We are constantly at work developing and refining our efforts through data collection, interviews and other tools.

Our programs have had a remarkable impact on communities across the nation. Also, our programs have been highlighted on CNN, ABC, NBC and other media outlets. As a result of our work, thousands of youth say they have been inspired to participate in community service, attend college or seek a form of technical training, avoid drug use, avoid gang activity and avoid other negative behavior.

Parents across the country have expressed their gratitude because our programs have made a positive impact on their family and community. Student grades have increased alongside the improvements in their behavior at school and home. It has been a struggle to achieve these results, but I have invested long hours and received little pay because I want to help change the world. There is nothing that I would rather do in this lifetime.

As I've mentioned before, my mother told me that if you want to change the world you have to first change yourself. The biggest and usually most difficult change a person will have to make is the change of self, but it's nearly impossible to change the world if you can't change yourself. As I grew I realized my mother was one of the wisest people I'd ever met, despite her plethora of abuses, and I've gained insurmountable amounts of insight through her actions and speech.

Sometimes having a rough past can callous a person. Though my mother never treated me kindly or spoke love toward me, she never preached or practiced hate either. Having a high level of hardship can indeed cause a person to respond negatively, but it can also create a desire to change the experience for someone else. It can create a level of compassion that yearns to overcome the hardships. I've seen so much killing, hatred and racism and all I want is the reverse. I was never attracted to the negativity, but I was attracted to problem solving and peace making. Since I've been exposed to what gangs, drugs, violence and a lack of education can do to a person, I want nothing but the polar opposite for the youth of today and the future.

Seeing how bad things were in India, back when I went on the breakdancing tour at fourteen, helped develop this passion that burns inside me today. Seeing the extreme poverty overseas was like receiving a *C-* on a paper and feeling bad, but seeing someone else get an *F*. It was bad. I'm running around in school with dirty shoes on, and before the trip I wanted a clean pair. Over there, they're running around barefoot with rags on. Really puts things into perspective. I knew I had to do something to help. For lack of better words, all I want to help do is turn weeds into roses so the whole world is a much more pleasant place.

The experience in India also developed a global vision for me. Most of the solutions that I wish I could impart on the world start locally, and the global approach starts with local problems. I might not have all the answers, but I know there's a solution out there to all the problems, and that solution lies in you. All you have to do is cultivate it and dig it out.

Looking back on things, I wish I could have done more to help my peers during my childhood. I've always wanted to help people, but back then I didn't know how to fulfill my wants. Pure inexperience mixed with fear (the great showstopper) of how to go about helping was what plagued me. Maybe I could have spoken up when someone was getting assaulted? Maybe I could have sacrificed my life so that someone else could live? Who knows what I could have done if I didn't have that cloud of fear? There have been times I've seen kids getting stomped by a group of guys with bats. Sure, I could have walked over and told them to stop, but I was too intimidated to speak up. For all I knew, my actions could have just caused them to beat us both instead of saving the victims.

Another factor that hindered me helping people early on was the sheer number of people needing help in that environment. It was daunting and it discouraged me, causing me to think that since I couldn't help everyone, who should I help? Now I know to go into every situation thinking that if I can't help everyone, who *can* I help?

An early photo of my twin brother Rodney, sister Kimberly
and myself (on the right)

More family times, this time my brother Rodney on the left, sister Pamela in the middle, myself on the right and in between my brother and I is my sister Kimberly.

In 1989 I became a member of the U.S. Army Reserves

Striking a pose while at Clark Atlanta University School of
Business

Enjoying dinner with my dad Fred, former wife Cecile and my beautiful mom Elizabeth.

In Tokyo, Japan, discussing global education strategy with
the Mayor of Akishima, Tokyo, Japan, Mr. Joichi Kitagawa
and a member of his staff.

Taking questions from students in Japan. What an amazing experience.

I've always loved coaching basketball. Here I am with a championship team.

The BEM Methodology, the core principles of our mission.

A photograph taken during my congressional run for office.

Our first Youth Town Hall event in Alexandria, VA

kicking off our 11-city tour.

On stage at the Youth Town Hall event discussing the importance of education.

Here I am sitting alongside students, faculty, entrepreneurs and community leaders at our Youth Town Hall event.

Media coverage for our events brought great awareness to the issues facing our youth.

A proud moment, our Power Texting Mentor Network
display launches in Best Buy in Alexandria, VA

Business owners and young people coming together for our Career Shadowing Program.

Checking in on our Career Shadowing participants at a Best
Buy in Alexandria, VA

What a night! Our corporate sponsor Capital One invited us to an NBA game.

Sharing a teachable moment during the game with some incredible young minds.

I barely recognize myself in this picture, taken during my long legal ordeal. I dropped over 25 pounds with all the stress, but still had to put my suit on and keep things moving.

I always love being in the community. Here I am at a
bilingual job fair in Alexandria, VA

Accepting the Celebrating Partnership Award at George Mason University between the BEM Foundation, Fairfax County School District and Bryant High School.

The Mitchell and Jackson men: (from left to right) my half-brother Bob, Dad, myself, half-brother Greg and twin brother Rodney. I love these guys!

FIVE

Bringing People Together - Hope

To lead is to lend a hand. Leadership has been defined as an act or instance of leading, guiding or giving direction. I believe that one cannot lead an organization or team of people, large or small, and demand respect, if he or she has not struggled or has never been denied success. Some believe that you must be willing to undertake the difficulties in life because it will force you to confront and overcome challenges.

Every human being on earth is born with gifts, talents and intangible tools. Vision and confidence are essential to achieve your dreams and overcome insurmountable circumstances like poverty. Whether you come from an underfunded school system, a drug-infested community or an uninspiring environment, I sincerely believe it can all be overcome, but you gotta be hungry!

You've read all I've endured, all of my obstacles, and you saw me overcome, but you have to be even hungrier. You have to overcome no matter what your problem is. At thirty, I was reading at a sixth or seventh-grade level, and I STILL made it into law school (graduated too). My math was around an eighth-grade level, not even past high school, but through it all I stayed hungry, and I kept going. And I did it.

Overcoming whatever is put in front of you is the most important thing you'll ever do, and it will always need to be done. Listen to an introduction for a boxer like Manny Pacquiao. Just digest how many titles he's won in different divisions, how much success he's had over the years. Everyone expects him to win. All the odds are in his favor. No one even thinks about the guy he's fighting because Manny has all the credentials to pull away with a victory, but that's what I had to face and that's what you have to face. It's little ol' you versus Manny, and you have to overcome. I had to knockout the champ with just my heart. My training wasn't as good, my hands weren't as big and my arms weren't as strong. I lacked the resources, lacked a father growing up, had a learning disability, lacked a proper education, but despite all that I brought him down. How? I have God, heart and hunger on my side. Whatever your position, whatever your situation, whatever your obstacle, you have got to keep fighting until you win. Get hungry and stay hungry.

Hunger can be defined as a compelling desire or craving. If you are hungry it doesn't matter if you attend a public school. If you are hungry it doesn't matter if your mother is a single parent or if you live in a low-income, drug and gang-infested community. If you are hungry it doesn't matter if your parents don't have the financial resources to fund your college education. If you are hungry it doesn't matter if your father is never around and if he is not supportive or loving. If you are hungry failure will not be an option. If you are hungry the desire to succeed will always outweigh your fear of failure. If you are hungry it doesn't matter if you are African American, Caucasian, Asian, Latino or mixed with all four, your focus will feature success. If you are hungry it doesn't matter if you are Christian, Muslim, Buddhist or Jewish. If you are hungry, it doesn't matter if you are rich or poor. If you are hungry you will learn from yesterday, embrace today and seek tomorrow. If you are hungry it doesn't matter what your current circumstances are, you will find a way or make a way to become successful.

A young man named Lance was preparing to try out for his high school basketball team and expressed to his dad an interest in becoming an NBA star one day. His dad introduced him to a coach Barnes.

The coach spoke with the player for a few minutes and said, "Meet me at the park on the basketball court at 5:30 am tomorrow."

Lance was at the court at 5:30, waiting patiently for Coach Barnes, but the coach didn't show up until 9am. "You ready?" the coach asked, smirking.

"Yes, sir, I'm ready to get started." Lance rubbed his palms together in anticipation.

"Great!"

But instead of playing basketball, the pair proceeded to walk for miles until they arrived at a beach. The coach sauntered up to a small boat, pushed it into the water and climbed in before starting to row.

"Come on into the water, Lance."

Lance listened and waded out until the coach held up a hand to stop the aspiring star. The water was to Lance's knees. After a brief pause, the coach motioned Lance forward, holding up a hand when the water was at Lance's chin. The coach paddled closer to Lance until they were an arm's distance apart.

"One more step," the coach said, leaning over the side of the boat.

Lance obeyed, submerging his head for a few seconds before attempting to surface. But before his nose could break the water, the coach pushed down Lance's head and held him under. The coach lightened the grip and let Lance take a breath before shoving the boy back under. Lance fought with all his might, kicking and flailing his arms until white foam frothed the area and the boat rocked. Moments before Lance slipped into unconsciousness, the coach yanked the boy aboard. As the boy gagged and coughed, struggling to breath, his eyes wide with fear, the coach smiled.

"When you were underwater, what did you desire the most?"

"Air?" Lance said, shoulders still heaving. "I thought I was going to die and all I wanted was to breathe."

"If your desire and fight to be an NBA superstar is greater than your desire to breathe, I promise you will be successful."

In other words you must be willing to sacrifice your last breath to achieve your goals and live your dreams no matter what. Simply put you gotta be hungry!

As a volunteer, I have coached basketball and other sports for years within different communities across America. Some people are naturally gifted with athletic ability and others possess very little. I have noticed that the most gifted students and athletes can be lazy, relying on their gift to progress them in sports and academics. They typically don't have the work ethic or desire because most of what they choose to pursue is effortless. I learned that athletes and students with lesser gifts work twice as hard and don't rely on their gifts because they can't. As a result, they have a greater desire to succeed and are typically hungrier than their gifted friends. I believe that if you find your passion, you will have the fuel to fulfill your purpose in life.

> What a man is driving is not important; it's what is driving the man...
>
> - Unknown

Most successful people talk openly about their success, but rarely discuss their failure or what drove them to acquire their motivation. What inspired them to fly so high and soar to new heights? What was the wind beneath their wings, the one element that pushed them to excel and overcome any obstacle in their path? No one talks about it but I believe the key to success is hidden in the failures.

Let's make it happen, U.S. Congress, VA

During the fall of 2010, I decided to run for U.S. Congress in the 8th District of Virginia. As a Democrat, I believe in the dream Dr. Martin Luther King Jr. spoke of for many years before his death in 1968. For years I have worked in several communities across America. In each, I have tried to make a contribution that would improve the life of others, whether it was donating money, time or volunteering. There has always been a need and desire to serve my community and the nation, and throughout my life I have tried to do both.

I moved to Virginia to work as a management consultant for Booz Allen Hamilton in January 2007. I resided in Falls Church, Virginia, for a few years. During this period I begin to spend a lot of my time working as a mentor and volunteer basketball coach. It was fun, and I was able to work with hundreds of kids and families. As a child growing up in Chicago I played sports all throughout the year because it was an outlet that helped keep me out of trouble. I worked with several volunteer coaches from different nationalities. They were instrumental in my life and helped to mold my attitude at a very vital time.

To improve or shape a community you must work

with youth. It is their behavior that will determine the value of the neighborhood. The more time that I spent in the community, the more I learned about how families were being underserved. I wanted to help bring real change to the community. I continued to work with youth and speak with parents and look for solutions. I realized the answer was hidden within the community, but many residents didn't have a voice. The community was becoming more diverse by the day; however, opportunities and resources didn't mirror the evolution of the population. Every day new issues were presented to local leadership. Issues involving education, transportation, employment and healthcare. I was so invested in the community that many people came to me for answers. They believed that I had the answers because of my common-sense approach to problem solving.

The more I traveled throughout Northern Virginia and met with residents, the more people expressed their concerns for my safety. Virginia has had a negative reputation for their treatment of African Americans in leadership, education, business and the criminal justice system for hundreds of years. Many have witnessed the harsh treatment President Obama received since he was elected and believed that I too would be subjected to similar hatred and racism.

Despite growing concerns I developed a roadmap that I thought could improve Northern Virginia. I shared my vision with hundreds of people and was asked to consider running for U.S. Congress. I prayed to God about running for a political office because I never had a desire to get involved with politics before. To me, there appeared to be a lot of fighting between the two parties without any sustainable solutions. I admired certain qualities about certain politicians like Abraham Lincoln and Ronald Regan. Although they both led America during two different eras and made separate contributions, they have made a lasting impact on my life.

Inspired by the spirit of our forefathers and the community at large, I decide to go ahead and run for the U.S. Congress as a Democrat. I received several calls from different people entrenched in the Democratic Party, asking me not to run against Jim Moran. Additionally, I met with leadership in Fairfax County, Virginia, and they too urged me to me run as an Independent candidate. I was also asked to consider running as a Republican, but I declined the offer.

It was a completely unforgettable, true experience.

Although I had gained some exposure about the political process through a training program at the Sorensen Institute for Political Leadership, nothing could prepare me for what I was about to encounter.

I learned that despite the election of Barack Obama, race matters. Race breeds hatred for some and further exposes how little America has progressed in regards to race relations. I admire the president's courage and intestinal fortitude. In my opinion, his election was the biggest social impact in America since the Civil Rights movement. I am grateful that I could witness such a courageous act.

I was relatively unknown to most people in Northern Virginia, but they swiftly learned who I was because I was one of the few African-American candidates. It seemed like a good thing and people wanted to hear what I had to say about issues. They wanted to learn about my platform and vision for their region.

I traveled all around Northern Virginia visiting schools, churches and several outdoor occasions. My fundraising events were well supported and we raised money, but not enough to compete with U.S. Congressman Jim Moran. I participated in a few ride alongs with local police officers, which allowed me to visit several households in different communities. I gained a better insight and greater respect for public servants and the duties assigned to people holding a public office. I took this opportunity seriously and met thousands of people and listened to their stories. Each story provided me with the fuel that I needed to map out how we could help turn things around. Oftentimes my interactions were emotional because people were desperate and seeking solutions. Some of the people that I encountered had already given up, and others were on the brink of quitting. They had lost their hope and were struggling financially, emotionally and physically.

Throughout my career I have worked with people from all walks of life. I believe in diversity and what it has to offer. As a result I was able to assemble a good team of people relatively new to Virginia politics. They worked hard and volunteered many long hours, but it was not enough to get me on the ballot as a candidate for the U.S. Congress. I invested a lot of money, time and effort into the run, so it was a tough loss, but overall it was a great experience. I learned a lot and it helped lay the foundation for another opportunity that would change my life.

State Senate, VA

After the failed attempt to run for the U.S. Congress, I was emotionally exhausted and physically beat up due to the many sacrifices I had to make while seeking political office. I received several calls from different people asking if I would be interested in running for a State Senate seat. There was some redistricting in the 39th district, and they believed I could win.

Still exhausted from my congressional campaign, I thought long and hard about the opportunity. I decided to run, but the deadline had passed to be considered as the Democratic candidate so I had to run as an Independent. At that time, I had no clue I would be prey for the Democratic Party in Alexandria. In America there are two dominant political organizations: the Democratic and the Republican parties. The Independent party is an organization of people with no specific ties to either party. Independents are also the smallest among all political parties.

Time was running out, and I only had a few weeks to get the support I needed to get my name on the ballot. There were several organizations that were interested in my candidacy. I was contacted by a gentleman named Michael Piche, who said he was sent by a group of potential supporters that wanted to help me get the signatures I needed to get on the ballot. Considering we only had a few weeks to get 250 signatures, I welcomed his assistance. He said he would get all the signatures I needed.

When we neared the submission deadline he asked me to help him and a team of volunteers gather their remaining signatures to qualify. I originally agreed with the understanding that he would get what I needed and that I would not have to worry about getting signatures. I was familiar with some of the election laws; however, I knew very little as it relates to gathering signatures. During my U.S. congressional campaign, I had a great team and management. In this situation I didn't have either because it was understood that I would get everything I needed once I got on the ballot. Without giving his plea for my help much thought, I came out and assisted the volunteers in order to get a few signatures.

Prior to this event I had never committed a crime, been affiliated with any criminal activity or even been accused of committing a crime. I possessed an interim top secret clearance and devoted my life to serving others through community service, non-profit work and military service (my stint in the U.S. Army).

In August 2011, I contacted the state senate clerk's office and they informed me that my petitions were due in the next week if I wanted to run for the 2011 state senate election. I knew that I was under a time crunch, but I believed that we could meet the deadline and get on the ballot. The state senate clerk's office told me to submit all my documents by August 23, 2011, by 7pm, and that I could "amend" my application with any additional information after the August 23, 2011, 7pm deadline. I was informed that most candidates typically make mistakes with their applications.

The days leading up to August 23, 2011, were hectic and tiring. I had several people volunteer to help me with the last minute push for office. However, nobody could have predicted the events of August 23rd. August 23rd was the same day as an earthquake in the area.

Earthquakes aren't common in Virginia, so it was difficult to get around. Traffic was bad, several phone lines were inoperable and we were rushing to submit signatures from my petitions for the State Senate 39th District of Virginia to the Alexandria registrar office. The amount needed to be on the ballot for the general November 8, 2011, election was 250 signatures of registered voters in the 39th District of Virginia.

Prior to submitting the petitions on August 23, 2011, I was gathering my petitions for submission and called a volunteer named Cynthia Richardson, who had gathered signatures for me from her community. I asked about her location so I could get her petitions picked up. She was far away. Due to the traffic and other issues caused by the earthquake, I was unable to meet with her in person to get the original signed petition to submit by the 7pm deadline. Cynthia Richardson had the original petition and it was my mistaken belief that I could sign the petition with the names on her list and amend my application with the original petition at a later date. Because of this thought, I asked Cynthia to hold onto the original petition. I would have to submit it the next day so the Virginia board of elections would not think I had forged any signatures.

It was never my intent to defraud the system or break the law. I was under a major time crunch and I did what I thought was acceptable based on my knowledge of the rules and information I was given a week prior from the state senate clerk's office in Richmond, VA. After I submitted my petitions on August 23, 2011, I tried to reach Cynthia Richardson over the next few days, but was unsuccessful.

On Friday, August 26, I received a call from the

state senate clerk's office informing me that my file was incomplete. Information was missing, and they asked if I wanted to amend my file. I told them that I did have some additional information to submit. They faxed me some information to fill out, and in the interim I received a call and found out that a detective was asking questions about my petitions. I didn't know why they were doing so, but I thought it was part of the process to get on the ballot. Earlier in the week Tom Parkins called me from the registrar's office of Alexandria to inquire about some initials of the person that notarized my petitions. He never asked me about or informed me that there were any issues with my petitions.

During this time I made repeated attempts to contact Cynthia Richardson. On Saturday morning August 27, 2011, I finally spoke with her, and she informed me that she had fallen down the stairs, sustaining a concussion, and that was why she could not be reached. I asked her for the original petition so I could amend my application and validate the names she gave me from her petition. She informed me that she had accidentally thrown them away. Hearing her words felt like someone had snatched the wind out of my lungs. I asked if she remembered where could have thrown them away. She said she didn't remember where, so I thought it would be best if I withdrew from the race to sort things out.

The original petition had been thrown away, and it was no longer possible to validate the names she gave me from her petition and amend my application with the original petition. It was an awful mistake on her behalf, though she honestly thought I no longer needed the petitions.

I'm still at a loss as to why anyone would throw away a petition. Maybe it was a miscommunication between us. After all, an earthquake had just rocked the community a few hours prior.

It was not my intention to commit any unlawful act, and as soon as I could, on Monday at 8:15 A.M., August 29, 2011, I called the State Board of Election and the City of Alexandria's registrar office and had my name withdrawn from the race. Several weeks after the incident occurred I was informed again that I was being investigated, so I spoke with an attorney about the events.

A week later Detective Hoffmaster came by my home to inquire about my actions, but I made no comments about the case and directed him to an attorney that I had spoken with about the incident. After speaking with my first attorney again, I decided to hire another attorney. The day after I retained Marina Medvin, Esq., and before she could contact the district attorney to inform him that she was going to represent me regarding this matter, the police arrested me at my home and took me to the Alexandria police department for fingerprinting and processing.

It was a nightmare. I couldn't believe that I had been arrested. I didn't have a clue as to the mistakes and errors that were made. My attorney notified me that she had met with the Alexandria district attorney, Randy Segal, and that I had made several errors with my petitions, which I was not aware of during the entire process.

At my own fault I had relied on others to confer the correct information to me while rushing to meet the 7pm deadline. My lack of due diligence, the poor communication and poor understanding of the rules and procedures regarding election law caused me to make several poor decisions. It was not my intent to do anything illegal or malicious, but I know now that I made several mistakes. It was clearly poor judgment on my behalf. The entire process of getting on a ballot was overwhelming and more than I could handle. If I had not been rushing to meet the deadline, and if I had a better understanding about election laws and the entire process, I am certain that I would not have made such poor decisions.

I hoped and prayed that I would be given the opportunity to make right the wrong that I had committed. I was and am remorseful and I apologize for my conduct. It was never my intention to violate any laws. As a Christian I have devoted my life to serving and improving the lives of others. For twenty years I have worked with at-risk youth and families through community service, and I have tried to make an impact that will hopefully make the world a better place. My greatest fear from this incident was that I would not be able to continue to work with thousands of at risk youth and families, locally and across America.

During this period I was supporting the BEM Foundation (the non-profit organization that I founded years ago to help improve the lives of youth and families). I believed that the felony conviction they charged me with was harsh and would be devastating to my efforts. I made an error and believed that I should be held accountable by the court, but I did not agree that a felony conviction was due punishment. Unfortunately, most African Americans in this country are treated much harsher than their white counterparts.

Prior to this incident, I was considered, by many, to

be a well-educated, squeaky-clean male. They were treating a veteran of the U.S. Army, an entrepreneur and an educator with a passion for community development as some thug. The world we live in is filled with hatred and racism. Despite my neighborhood transformation work with police officers, organizations, churches, parents and schools, the prosecutors pursued me as though I had committed a drive-by shooting.

Some may ask if I was simply not ready to run for Congress and the Virginia State Senate. I mentioned it was rushed, but I don't think it was a mistake to run, nor do I regret running. I had been doing community service for years. Naturally, when a person engages in the community to help others, they fight in the trenches. To a certain extent, servants endure some of the hardships of the people they are serving. You can't pull a person out of a mud pit without getting a little dirty yourself. When a wife loses her husband to cancer, or a child in a gang shooting, I'm invested in their lives because they make up the community. It's only makes sense that I'd want to represent and serve these people in the government. My service in the community felt like a springboard to send me into the government to further the help I was already doing.

I bore a great responsibility to the community and

the thousands of kids and their families who depended on my efforts. I was and still am willing to give my life to save our youth. My only hope and prayer is that I am able to continue my work and make a difference in the lives of those who need it most.

Decades later, after all of the good work I have done, there are days when the harsh streets of Chicago seem like a distant memory. Still, the crossroads I experienced growing up in a gang and drug-infested community seem to be more present in my life than ever before. As a kid I tried my best to do the right thing and to make a difference, and as an adult I still share this philosophy.

My attorney, Marina Medvin, advised me to think long and hard about my plea decision and she gave me her expert opinion. It was a complicated decision, and I looked at it from three different perspectives. First, I was taught that if I made a mistake I had to be accountable for my actions.

Second, to ensure I didn't make any errors I sought out guidance from the state senate clerk's office in Richmond, Virginia. Third, my actions were based upon a misunderstanding of election laws and a mild impairment, which causes incidental memory and periodic lapses in vigilance, both due at least in part to organic factors that are beyond my control.

Unfortunately, I made several very poor choices. I wasn't aware that I had made a mistake until my attorney, Marina Medvin, and close friend, Earon William, an attorney, explained to me that I actually did make several errors. I couldn't believe it. I had tried my best to make no mistakes. Considering the aforementioned, I couldn't stand in front of jury and lie. I now recognized I *had* made an error, and I believe in transparency. I elected to plead guilty and requested a bench trial, which would allow my attorney to submit evidence and facts on my behalf in front of a judge and not a jury. I believed that Judge Kibbler would see the real reason why I was being prosecuted like a child molester.

This was the lowest point in my life, and I did more than consider suicide. I remember lying in my bed and thinking, "I'm just tired of being here." I just didn't want to be here anymore, but there was no feasible escape as long as I was alive. I was so afraid to face people, and I didn't really know who I was or why this was happening to me. I didn't want anybody to see me, I didn't want to talk to anybody and I didn't want to talk about it.

I closed my eyes and began to pray, and talk to my deceased mother, and cry and cry and cry. I mean, I was down to the point where I sat there, and I had this pair of scissors in my hand. I just kept sliding the blade on my wrist. I wasn't trying to go sideways. I was going vertical. I didn't want to be there at all. If I had more time, if the scissors weren't so dull, I think I would have followed through with it. I can't say for sure, but I was leaning toward that.

To make things worse, one day while I was driving from church I got a call from my lawyer, Marina Medvin. Ten days before my trial began my attorney said, "I can no longer represent you."

"What? Why?" I said, trying my hardest not to swerve as the adrenaline shook my hands.

"They're trying to send you to jail, and," somehow I could hear it in her voice that she was looking at the ground. "It's just wrong."

I was silent for a few seconds, my brain moving as fast as my car as I tried to process what she was saying. She continued before I could piece together a response.

"I've been having nightmares about this case. It hurts, Ron, it hurts bad to see what they're doing to you. I don't think I can hold up in court with this. You're a good person who's trying to make the world a better place. I admire what you're doing. The world needs more people like you." She sighed loudly. "Considering all the facts and your history, this situation is just too disturbing for me."

"I don't believe you," I said, still shaking but trying to keep the quake out of my voice. "What's really going on here? What's the real reason you can't represent me anymore?"

After a long pause and another loud sigh, "That is the real reason. I'm sorry, Ron."

I still didn't believe her, but I held my tongue. I thanked her and hung up, feeling as though I'd just driven off a cliff. There was a lot involved with my case, and I believed that she was just not experienced enough. However, she was professional and kind enough to introduce me to Ryan Campbell, a local attorney in Alexandria, Virginia, who had recently been named Trial Lawyer of the Year, 2011, in the Washington D.C. area.

She spoke highly of Ryan Campbell, and after meeting him I understood why. He was organized and overall a better lawyer. Although I had a new lawyer representing me, Marina Medvin's actions nearly destroyed my spirit. I trusted her with my life and she bailed out during a critical moment. I felt she did what was in her best interest instead of what was in the interest of her client.

When I was a child my mother shared many stories about African Americans being physically lynched from trees in Mississippi, and metaphorically lynched in the court room by White Americans throughout the country.

Regardless of the length of your life's journey, throughout the process you will need people to help you get through certain moments. My Pastor Don Hayes played a pivotal role in my spiritual growth, along with members of the Oakland Baptist Church. His prayers and guidance provided me with a foundation that I use today as a tool to help others dealing with adversity, to help them build a brighter future. Many of my close friends (like Kelly Gambrell, Carl Bandy, Lamar Brown and Ron Bell) provided me with unwavering words of encouragement and made several personal sacrifices to fuel my progress.

Kelly's constant prayers and inspiring words of wisdom helped me get through many nights and embrace the thought of a better day. Ron's spiritual guidance and inspiration gave me the power to persevere. The list could go on forever, but I think you get the gist, so I won't keep going. The point I'm making is that I am grateful to have such kind people in my life.

Additionally, working with my new attorney Ryan Campbell was very helpful. He was very supportive and understood the many challenges that stood ahead. Ryan helped to restore my faith through his hard work and due diligence, which I admire and thank him for to this date. To further combat the stress, I prayed a lot for strength and guidance. As a result I found this wonderful prayer, and it gave me strength:

MY LORD GOD, I have no idea where I am going. I do not see the road ahead of me. I cannot know for certain where it will end. Nor do I really know myself, and the fact that I think that I am following your will does not mean that I am actually doing so. But I believe that the desire to please you does in fact please you. And I hope I have that desire in all that I am doing. I hope that I will never do anything apart from that desire. And I know that if I do this you will lead me by the right road, though I may know nothing about it. Therefore will I trust you always, though I may seem to be lost and in the shadow of death. I will not fear for you are ever with me, and you will never leave me to face my perils alone. – Thomas Merton

On March 8, 2012, the morning of my court proceeding, I woke up around 6:00 A.M., stood up and fell immediately to my knees, too weak to support my weight. My eyes blurred with tears and my heart burned with discouragement. I grabbed my pillow and began to pray for strength, having no idea what was ahead of me.

I eventually gathered my composure and donned myself in a suit before driving to court. There, I went through security and met up with my attorney Ryan Campbell (and some witnesses for the case) for a few minutes. Subsequently, I entered the floor where my trial was being held.

As I approached the courtroom there was a crowd of people waiting to enter. I was humbled and overwhelmed by the large number of people present, and around 98 percent of those in attendance were there to support me. It was like watching an episode of *Law and Order*. The community came out in full force to support me and it was standing room only in the court. The judge entered the courtroom and the trial began at 11:31 A.M. The following event took place:

THE COURT: Okay. Mr. Campbell, have you had an opportunity to review the pre-sentence investigation report with your client?

MR. CAMPBELL: We have, your Honor. There's no additions or changes to make.

THE COURT: Okay. Then I'll make the pre-sentence investigation report a part of the record. I did receive and I did read the Commonwealth's sentencing memorandum, the memorandum in aid of sentencing filed on behalf of Mr. Mitchell, and all the attachments to both. And then I did receive, I think yesterday or the day before, a copy of the neuropsychological evaluation that was performed I think in April of 2000 on Mr. Mitchell. And I think that was everything that was submitted.

MR. CAMPBELL: That's correct, your Honor.

THE COURT: Okay. Does either side have any evidence to present?

MR. CAMPBELL: Your Honor, I would just ask that the Court hear from two very brief witnesses in this case. The first witness is Ryan Prucker, your Honor.

WHEREUPON, RYAN PRUCKER WAS CALLED AS A WITNESS BY AND ON BEHALF OF THE

DEFENDANT AND, AFTER HAVING BEEN FIRST DULY SWORN, WAS EXAMINED AND TESTIFIED AS FOLLOWS:

DIRECT EXAMINATION BY MR. CAMPBELL:

Q. Mr. Prucker, could you just tell the judge your name and what you do for a living?

A. Certainly. My name is Ryan Prucker. I'm the president and owner of Imagelight Advertising and Production.

Q. Okay. Do you know Ronald Mitchell?

A. Yes, I do.

Q. Can you describe for the judge how long you've known him and how you know him?

A. Certainly. I met Ron over three years ago. I was taken by his foundation and some of the work that he had been doing in the community. I instantly wanted to get involved, to help some of his efforts using the skills that I have in marketing and public relations, and the ways that I might be able to help advance what he was doing.

And over that time period, we quickly became friends. I was really overwhelmed by his character and how giving he was, both in the foundation that he runs as well as personally, as a friend, and just observing him within the community, working with elderly, working with young kids, and even beyond the foundation work that might be promoted or publicly seen.

Just seeing the private things that he does, too, whether it be helping the elderly clean up after themselves and helping, making sure that students are constantly in contact with them, making sure that they're keeping up with their schooling and their grades, and providing supplies if need be, working with parents. All of that became very apparent the more and more that I got to know him as a person.

Q. You work with him in the BEM Foundation. Can you tell the court what his contributions are to that?

A. Sure. Ron is the foundation. It's his vision, it's his mission, it's his passion. And that involves creating and scheduling and organizing youth town hall events, both in Alexandria as well as across the country, youth mentoring opportunities, using technology to connect youth with mentors. So it's his passion, it's his -- he is the foundation.

Q. Okay. The last thing I want to ask you is, you've read the pre-sentence investigation report in this case. You understand what the Commonwealth's case was against Ronald Mitchell; you know what his involvement is. Can you tell me about the campaign, what you personally observed of how the campaign got started and what Ronald did with it?

A. I mean, actually, the campaign, I would surmise, or I would sort of say, is, it was almost over before it started. We are in the midst of working on -- we had just gotten done with a youth town hall event in Alexandria, and all of a sudden it was like "Hey, there's this opportunity."

It was, like, within days before the deadline to get on the ballot, and it was this call that "Hey," there was some support, maybe we could make this happen, maybe this would be -- the idea had been talked about as this would be the next way for him to get out into the community.

And so it was very hastily done. It was like "Okay, we need to" -- and there was no campaign manager, there was no platform other than what Ron believes. And it was very much like "Okay, let's just -- I got to figure out how to get on the ballot within a few days." And I guess there was some support that was supposed to be coming, but again, it was just -- it was very, very haphazard.

Q. And what was the hope after Ronald would be placed on the ballot? What was the plan?

A. Oh, sure. Well, then, that would be -- the plan is like, getting on the ballot would just be -- allow him the opportunity to now say "Okay, let's see how he can create a campaign and a platform," and all of those different things. But it all happened very fast. There wasn't -- the overall idea would be that that would be when we would start, Ron and anybody else who would be willing to support him would go out and help him campaign.

Q. Okay. Mr. Prucker, that's all I have for you. The commonwealth might have a couple questions for you.

A. Certainly.

CROSS EXAMINATION BY MR. SENGEL:

Q. Sir, how long have you known Mr. Mitchell?

A. About over three years.

Q. So you knew him when he tried to run for Congress against Jim Moran?

A. Yes.

Q. Did you help him with that campaign?

A. I did nothing proactively to help him other than a friend that said "Hey, that's great. I think it sounds great."

Q. Did you help him collect signatures or anything?

A. I did not.

Q. Did you have any discussions with him about that campaign, about the intents of it, and about how he was carrying it out?

A. No, I didn't.

Q. Your profession is in advertising and marketing, is that correct?

A. That's correct, sir.

Q. Do you provide those services to Mr. Mitchell's foundation? And if so, do you do them pro bono or do you charge him for it?

A. It's actually been a mixture of both. Initially it was *pro bono*, and then over time, as certain resources were necessary, there were certain production or other items that were for a fee.

Q. Do you have any idea over the course of the past year how much income your firm has derived from them?

A. I think it would probably be within the -- I would say 3,500 dollar range.

MR. SENGEL: That's all I have.

THE COURT: Anything further?

MR. CAMPBELL: Nothing further, your Honor.

THE COURT: Okay. Thank you very much.

THE WITNESS: Thank you.

MR. CAMPBELL: The second brief witness, your Honor, will be Earon Williams.

WHEREUPON, EARON WILLIAMS WAS CALLED AS A WITNESS BY AND ON BEHALF OF THE DEFENDANT AND, AFTER HAVING BEEN FIRST DULY SWORN, WAS EXAMINED AND TESTIFIED AS FOLLOWS:

DIRECT EXAMINATION BY MR. CAMPBELL:

Q. First, Mr. Williams, could you just tell the judge your name and your occupation?

A. Earon Williams, and I'm an in-house counsel for Geico.

Q. How long have you known Ronald Mitchell, and how do you know him?

A. I've known Ron since probably the late '90s, so maybe about fifteen, maybe a little less than fifteen years. We met in law school. I was in Pittsburgh. He was actually going to

University of Pittsburgh and I was at Duquesne. And I was a third year, and I think he was a 1L at the time.

Q. Okay. Can you describe for the court what you witnessed of Ron during this -first of all, what have you witnessed of Ron during this prosecution as far as remorse and his regret? How has this affected him?

A. Well, I think the first thing -- I think there's a ton of stress, I think understandable, throughout this entire process. But the one thing I can say from the beginning, once he gave me a call, was really the lack of understanding as far as the gravity of what's taking place, as far as what was done.

Several conversations that we had earlier on were just him saying -- trying to understand exactly what was being investigated, exactly his role, exactly what he should have or shouldn't have done, and for me to say "Listen, Ron, this is," kind of "what's going on. This is what took place, and this is kind of the direction it's going."

And really, the not only remorse, but just the reality that someone that's in that type of community service did something to not only let himself down but to let others down. So it was coming from a lot of different angles. As a friend, you try to be there as a friend, but also understanding as someone that's active in the community, there's a feeling of "I've done something, not only to wrong the community, but maybe to not necessarily cast myself in the most positive light."

Q. Can you tell the Court what, if any, emotional impact you've witnessed in Ron, or what physical impact, or mental impact, this case has had on him?

A. Physically, we were actually just talking about this the other day. Physically, he's lost a lot of weight. And I mean, that's just aesthetic, but I think that -- physical, just the stress of it all.

But then going back to law school, and even up until this point, there was always a, I don't want to call it a disconnect, but to a certain extent there's a disconnect that's always been present, and it really wasn't until recently that I've really been able to kind of complete the puzzle as far as some of the issues that may have been present. And some things I would talk to Ron about, and he would be remorseful, but at the same point he really didn't quite understand exactly what was actually done wrong about -- and for me, I can put on my legal hat and say "Well, this is what's going on." Personally, I wish I probably would have been a little more proactive, but trying to explain and then trying to understand and explain to him where the disconnect might be, to see -- you know, sometimes some things that might seem to be very clear to me, there was an obvious disconnect. And trying to understand that process and communicate with him as a friend, but at the same time also as a colleague, too. I'm not sure if that's answering your question.

Q. I think that does offer some -- shed some light on Mr. Mitchell. The Commonwealth might have some questions to follow up.

A. Sure.

MR. SENGEL: No questions.

THE COURT: Okay. Thank you very much, Mr. Williams.

MR. CAMPBELL: No other witnesses, your Honor.

THE COURT: All right. Any additional argument?

MR. SENGEL: Your Honor, I would just briefly say, I think the issue that's before the Court at this point is fairly clear. I think if the Court accepts the defendant's assertion that he's here today because he didn't understand what the law requires of him, or if he was confused and ill-informed and made mistakes which he didn't intend to make -- you know, if the Court believes that, then obviously that mitigates the outcome of this proceeding.

But I think in order for the Court to accept that assertion, you essentially have to turn a blind eye to a lengthy list of occurrences from which, I think, you can only draw one conclusion. And that is that Mr. Mitchell understood what the law required and he made a conscious decision to circumvent those requirements and he swore falsely under oath to try and cover it up.

The bottom line in this case, I think, is that the requirements for filing voter signature petitions are clearly stated on the forms in language that is clear and easily understood by a person of average intelligence, and I think to the extent that the neuropsychological evaluation which was done on Mr. Mitchell over ten years sheds any light on this case, it certainly concludes that his global intellectual functioning is within the average or low average range.

But in addition to that, I think the Court cannot ignore the fact that, even assuming there is some impairment or some difficulty there, obviously, Mr. Mitchell was able to overcome those, and he attained advanced degrees in the field of law, in the field of business, and by some account became the president of a foundation, the CEO of a consulting firm.

So clearly, whatever's going on there did not impair his ability to do well and accomplish a good deal. I think the requirements that he claims to have misunderstood certainly would be comprehensible to anyone with his educational background and his prior experience having run for office.

And I think, as indicated in our memorandum, this is not the first time that Mr. Mitchell has had to collect and submit signatures on petitions to run for office. And I think to claim unfamiliarity and confusion about the process, in light of that experience, is a questionable claim.

I think it's obvious from all these circumstances that, for whatever reason, Mr. Mitchell chose to disregard the legal requirements that he should have adhered to. The fact that he was in a hurry is not an excuse. I think his claim that he was struggling to meet the minimum number of 250 required signatures and that that was hampered somehow by the events of August 23rd, which was the day of the earthquake in Northern Virginia, simply don't ring true.

I mean, if you look at the petitions he filed, he filed a total of thirty-two of them. Twenty-five of these were completed and notarized the day before, on August 22nd, and those in and of themselves contained over 430 signatures.

And I think the claim that signing the voter's name on a petition himself is a misunderstanding is a bit of a stretch. Asking a voter to sign his wife's name on a petition is not a misunderstanding of what's required. Having other people collect signatures who are not qualified to collect signatures and then swearing under oath that he, himself, collected them -- again, that's just not a misunderstanding of what was required.

I think these were deliberate acts of deception, carried out in an attempt to advance his own agenda, to achieve a position of prominence, and to get on the ballot for a state senate seat.

At the end of the day, one might be tempted to say "Well, you know, okay. So what? He didn't get on the ballot, no harm, no foul." I don't think it's appropriate to force that case into that kind of analysis, because I think, fundamentally, what Mr. Mitchell did undermines the public confidence in our system of government.

But I think, really, what's worse than that, given what Mr. Mitchell purports to do with his foundation, it is a much worse form of hypocrisy and it sets a terrible example for the young people that Mr. Mitchell purports to be interested in motivating and inspiring in his work. And I think the last thing in the world that those folks need to hear is that there are no real serious consequences for this kind of behavior.

And for those reasons, for all of these reasons, I would urge the Court to impose a sentence consistent with the recommendation in our memorandum.

THE COURT: Okay. Thank you, Mr. Sengel. Mr. Campbell?

MR. CAMPBELL: Your Honor, I hope that all courts, and certainly this court, starts with the basic premise when it sentences any individual that there is some wisdom in understanding that individual and their behavior before we impose a sanction for that misbehavior.

I understand that in most cases it will be impractical to really know the defendant, but in this case there are several things that I think stand out about Mr. Mitchell that I would wager no defendant has presented to this court in the past. First of all, he has achieved many great things, and perhaps there have been defendants who have achieved those same things that have come before this court, but when you take it in the context of where he came from it's simply astounding that he has gotten to the point where he is in his life.

The third thing that I hope is clear from the sentencing memorandum, and all the letters that have been submitted on his behalf, is that it is evident that Mr. Mitchell was motivated purely and primarily by his true and sincere desire to help people. That is his nature, and it apparently always has been his nature.

This case is unlike any other case this court has seen. First of all, it's a non-guidelines offense. Secondly, my understanding is that there has never been a prior prosecution in this jurisdiction for this offense. The only thing that comes close, in my recollection, is Mr. Moran's prosecution, where it appears from media accounts that he actually did financially benefit from his acts and ended up walking away with a misdemeanor offense and no jail time.

I think that ought to add some context to what we're doing in this case, where the only thing Mr. Mitchell was trying to do was get on the ballot and simply submit his name on the ballot. He had no financial gain to make, and really no personal gain, and really there was no gain claim to this whatsoever.

But Mr. Mitchell, as I think is evident, is unlike any

other defendant the court has seen. I think the neuropsychological evaluation is tremendously important because I think it documents that gap that Mr. Williams spoke about between Mr. Mitchell's -- what we see in Mr. Mitchell.

He's very polished, he's very articulate, he's very motivated, and he's achieved a lot of things, but there is a gap between that and the tremendous understanding and true ignorance that I think is, at its core, probably because he simply had no foundation growing up in Chicago and going to school, when he walks away with a -- as a high school graduate, being able to read at a fifth grade level, and about a decade later when he's in law school an evaluation comes back that he can now read at an eighth grade level, I think that speaks to his core, that he has some core -- whether it's organic, as is suggested in the neuropsychological evaluation, or whether it's simply that he never had the tools that many other people had growing up, I don't think that can really, honestly be disputed.

Growing up, it's evident in what Mr. Mitchell has told me that his government was failing him and his neighborhood. The police were infected, the schools were infected, and that was a matter of fact for him. Routinely neighbors were committing crimes against neighbors, including violent crimes and murder. The community was blighted by drugs and the police had no influence over anybody's behavior, and it was Mr. Mitchell who stepped up as a teenager and as a young boy and who actually made a positive impact, who began -- that's how his life sort of begins.

Nobody else is making a difference around him. He starts investing himself as a boy and a teenager to make a difference. And that has been his core principle his entire life.

I recounted the story that he's told me regarding the young man who robs him on the street and he invites him over for dinner the next week, but those stories -- Mr. Mitchell could frankly go on for days recounting those experiences that he had growing up.

And even though he could barely read at a fifth grade level graduating high school, because he had these values in himself, and because he wanted to -- he realized that in order to be effective and help all the individuals around him, he had to achieve these other things in his life. That was his primary motivating factor.

Your Honor, I think this is a case where I believe there's a vast difference -- it's evident there's a vast difference in our individual views of what's reasonable in this case, but I will point out that the Office of Probation and Parole has a recommendation, not for actual jail time, not even for suspended jail time. It's essentially, without naming it, a recommendation for what the defense is asking for in this case: an opportunity for Mr. Mitchell to simply continue doing what he's doing, investing in his community, as a consequence for what he's done in this case.

Your Honor, I think the waters are a little muddy here, in that there were many, many offenses the Commonwealth could have brought against Mr. Mitchell, and he ultimately pled guilty to one offense. That one offense really has never been fleshed out as to what act it was.

In Mr. Mitchell's mind, he simply didn't understand how he could collect that many signatures and sign the ballot, so he did have people working for him. And in fact, in the Commonwealth's investigation, many of those people say "Well, that's not my signature, but I gave somebody authority to sign for me" or "Well, that's not my signature, but I did sign a document." So there are some things here that I think corroborate that Mr. Mitchell simply didn't have an understanding of how to get this done.

I think it all goes back to what Mr. Prucker says regarding "it was over before it even started." This took about three days. It was off the cuff "Hey, let's try to get your name on the ballot and see what happens." And that was the context there. And on the last day, the people that are collecting signatures for Mr. Mitchell, there's an earthquake that occurs, traffic is gridlocked, phones go down, he's in a panic on how to get things submitted, so he does it the best way he can. And certainly he broke at least one law in doing that. How many, there's no agreement to.

I think it is notable that the Office of Probation and Parole make no recommendation for active incarceration, make no recommendation for suspended sentence, and even no recommendation for supervised probation. In essence, it is a recommendation that the court grant an SIS in this case.

Your honor, the appropriate sentence -- obviously, it's purely up to the Court at this point. I would ask that the Commonwealth -- that the Court be cautious of the Commonwealth's statement that, notwithstanding the defendant's previous accomplishments, it is important for the Court to focus on the conduct underlying this offense and the defendant's explanation for it.

Your Honor, this case, I think, ought to rest purely

on who Mr. Mitchell is, because not only is it astounding how great his failure was in this case, but I think it's explained in his history, in his growing up, in the lack of foundation that he had in his education, and in the psychological evaluation. You understand that he is lacking in some really fundamental things that other people have, and it does explain his conduct in this case.

Your Honor, Mr. Mitchell's remorse and mental state and shame in this case are enormous.

THE COURT: Can I just ask you a question? There was something that was set forth in the Commonwealth's sentencing memo that wasn't addressed at all, I don't think, by you in your sentencing memo about the statement of economic interest which Mr. Mitchell was required to file in which he was asked to list each employer that pays him a salary or wages in excess of 10,000 dollars annually, in which he listed BEM Foundation, as if they were paying him 10,000 dollars a year, at least.

MR. CAMPBELL: Your Honor, in speaking to Mr. Mitchell, my understanding is that, first of all, he didn't comprehend, I don't think, the document he was filling out. But when he -- when it says "more than 10,000," I think he thought "If I'm making any money from this foundation," basically "up to and including 10,000 dollars," that's why he checks the box. He wasn't making -- he never made 10,000 dollars from this foundation. He has perhaps made a few thousand, but I would even doubt that. But certainly never more than 10,000 dollars, and it is not a vehicle for which he's getting rich or profiting that greatly.

THE COURT: No, I'm not suggesting it was. It's just that it wasn't accurate, it wasn't truthful.

MR. CAMPBELL: Your Honor, I wouldn't say that it was a lie or untruthful. It's not accurate, but I believe that Mr. Mitchell just didn't understand the point of the question, "How much are you making?" He believed that if he was making up to 10,000 dollars, that he needed to disclose that and that's what he did, rather than err on the side of underestimating how much he was making.

Your Honor, first I agree with the Commonwealth that this, the shame that he feels, is because he feels that he has let so many people down. Young people, the older people, all the people that he's helped in his life and all the people that look to him. It's a source of shame for him. And your Honor, he's lost weight. He's shed countless tears. And he's gone through many sleepless nights.

The thing that most, perhaps, sheds some light on

the level of disappointment and shame that Mr. Mitchell feels is because he's dedicated his life to helping other people. The other day in my office he said to me that he believed that he had let God down. And that was something he couldn't even articulate the feeling of letting God down in his life. But that's the enormity of the shame that he feels over these acts, and the disappointment that he's brought to himself and other people.

Your Honor, in a more practical way, I think Mr. Mitchell obviously fears greatly that he's not going to be able to lead the BEM Foundation. That's a primary way he's defined his life in the past couple of years. That's the thing that's centered in his life at this point. They rely on corporate sponsorship, and of course having a person with a felony conviction is not going to be practical for the success of the corporation, so that's something that he's quite concerned about.

Your Honor, he's shared with me the tremendous irony that he's gone so many years growing up in his Chicago neighborhood without having a criminal record when all the other people around him never made it out of high school one way or the other, whether it's going to prison or being killed or becoming addicted to drugs or alcohol. He's made it this far, only to do this and subject himself to that label. It's tremendously disappointing and shameful to him.

Your Honor, the Commonwealth's characterization of Mr. Mitchell, I think, is quite inaccurate. First of all, he's never held public office. He is not in any way a professional politician. He's never worked for a politician. He's never worked in a government office. He doesn't know the first thing about running a campaign, except that he's got to get his name on the ballot.

The only thing that he does share, I think, with politicians is that he's tremendously inspired, he's inspiring to other people, and he's got a dream of how to improve the world. In fact, his only platform that he ever articulated when he was trying to get on the ballot as an independent is "I want to help other people." That's his political platform.

Your Honor, we know the Commonwealth's position as to whether the act was committed, and I agree that it comes purely down to whether the Court accepts the defendant's position here, and it certainly would be mitigating. But I think all these things that we know about Mr. Mitchell do shed some light and corroborate his misunderstanding about this case.

Your Honor, I was hoping -- the neuropsychological

evaluation arrives at its own conclusions. There's many different test instruments. Unfortunately, the one doctor is now deceased. We're not in a position to hire another evaluator, but I think the evaluation is self-explanatory for the most part. I would just point out a few things.

First, it talks about whether it's an organic deficiency or a parietal lobe dysfunction. One or the other, Mr. Mitchell suffers from something that is a learning disability for him. It hampers his basic problem solving ability. It doesn't allow him to learn as well as others.

And I can share with the Court that when Mr. Mitchell went through law school, he didn't just go to class and listen to the lecture and read the book and understand the case. He had to go through this enormous process where he was dedicating eighteen hours a day to learning what other people could probably learn in three or four hours. He's got to read the case multiple times, he's got to rewrite the case. He's got to speak it out orally, and then he's got to listen to it on tape.

And that's how hard he's working to make it through and achieve the things that he's done. Your Honor, I would ask the Court to really -- first, the Commonwealth hasn't put forth what the appropriate sentencing theory is here.

They've said that there's some harm to the community, but that's speculative. The harm to the community is that he's going to get his name on the ballot and take away votes from somebody else. I don't think there's really much to support that.

He derived no financial gain whatsoever from this, and in fact would only have been working harder had he been nominated to the ballot and they would have really had to work it out for him. And also keep in mind that the Commonwealth has already pointed out that there weren't enough registered voters. If you went through all those names and got rid of the ones that -- had they been properly submitted, there wouldn't have been enough to get him on the ballot.

Your Honor, there's certainly no reason to incapacitate Mr. Mitchell. There's no purpose for rehabilitation here at all. What's the retribution? What is the harm done to the community? There is none. And the only deterrence, besides Mr. Mitchell, is the audience of people that are here to support him. The only people that a harsh sentence would be deterring are the people that know Mr. Mitchell and know what he's going through right now.

Jail is totally unwarranted, your Honor. And I'm

asking for no more than what the Court of Appeals has authorized. A suspended imposition of sentence merely means that the Court's pronouncement of sentence is that there is no sentence. The case gets set for a future date, and at that point, upon certain conditions, the defendant is discharged.

There's nothing else that the Court of Appeals has authorized, and that's simply what we're asking for. I point out that the Epps case is still pending in the Supreme Court, so whether or not the Court of Appeals is correct in Epps is still to be decided. But clearly, there's authority for the SIS right now through Epps, and the court merely pronounces the sentence that there is no sentence, and the case gets set out for conditions in the future.

I think that is the absolute right thing to do in this case, given Mr. Mitchell's unique circumstance in this case.

THE COURT: Okay. Thank you, Mr. Campbell. Mr. Mitchell, is there anything else you'd like to say at this time?

THE DEFENDANT: Yes, Ma'am. I know what I want to say.

THE COURT: That's all right. Just take your time. Do you want Mr. Campbell to read your written statement?

THE DEFENDANT: I know what I want to say. I wrote it down. Your Honor, I want to sincerely apologize for my poor judgment. I'm very remorseful and I take it very seriously. I've been very ill as a result of this. I've dedicated my life to serving people in the community. I've talked to a thousand kids and parents about making bad decisions. And unfortunately, I made a poor decision.

And now I don't know what to say. I'm very sorry, and I ask for your grace and your mercy. Please give me the opportunity to the make the wrong that I've done right, and allow me to continue helping, to serve God. That's all I want to do. Nothing else.

THE COURT: Okay. All right. Thank you, Mr. Mitchell. Is there any reason why the court should not sentence you at this time?

MR. CAMPBELL: No, your Honor.

THE COURT: Okay. Well, Mr. Mitchell, I will -- I do want to compliment you on all your accomplishments. Given where you came from and where you ended up before getting here today, it's truly astounding. And it's impressive. Not only were you successful in getting an undergraduate degree, but you went on and pursued a law degree, a business degree, you started a foundation. And you have done -- no question, you have given back to the community in which you're living, and it's clear that you have certainly been an inspiration to a lot of young people and their families, and as attested to by Mr. Prucker, helped the elderly.

And it's very impressive, and I think that's what makes this all so much more disappointing. And clearly you've disappointed yourself and those who know you and have worked with you, your friends. It's hugely shocking and disappointing.

The neuropsychological evaluation that was provided by counsel, that was performed while you were in law school -- I think it was while you were a freshman in law school -- while perhaps it sheds some light, it does indicate that you are of average intelligence, and that your ability to exercise appropriate judgment in certain social situations is pretty much average, although it talks about there being some sort of core deficits. And perhaps, Mr. Williams, over the fifteen years or so that he's gotten to know you, has seen some of that.

But what is clear is that the face of the petitions that you were asking people to sign, or that you had other people take around to sign, to get the right number of signatures that you needed, was so clear and so obvious to anybody, but especially somebody with even your level of training, intelligence, and education, that you had to personally witness -- or the person who was signing, their signature had to be personally witnessed.

You had to so state under oath that you personally witnessed the signatures. And it couldn't have been clearer. So it's hard to accept that you didn't understand that. It is hard to accept that. And it's hard to understand that you didn't understand what the law required of you in light of the fact that, in 2010, you did attempt to run for the United States Senate. So you weren't new to the process, even though you had a very short timeframe in which to try to get your name on the ballot for this last state election.

Whether you made a conscious decision to violate the law, or whether you intended to violate the law, you know that in your heart. And it's just a very unfortunate occurrence in what really, up to this point, has been a pretty stellar life for you.

That all being said, I think that the stigma of a felony conviction and all that that entails is significant punishment. I don't think this is a case for an SIS. This is a case of fraud, where Mr. Mitchell was or wanted to be a candidate seeking public office, but was essentially, by his conduct, betraying the public's trust from the very beginning.

And when one considers Mr. Mitchell's level of education and reputation in the community, it just is not an appropriate case for an SIS. He pled guilty in December of last year, and the court found him guilty. But as I said, the stigma of a felony conviction is a significant punishment in this matter and for Mr. Mitchell, and will be.

The Court, having found you guilty of election fraud, will impose a sentence of twelve months, with all twelve months suspended, and require that you complete one year of supervised probation, and during the course of that probation complete 100 hours of community service, which is probably a drop in the bucket for you, Mr. Mitchell. Community service is really your thing. And you also have to pay your court costs, all right? So when you leave court today, you need to go directly over to the probation department, and they can do an intake.

MR. CAMPBELL: Thank you, your Honor.

THE COURT: All right. Good luck, Mr. Mitchell.

Many people believed that if every event involving my case would have been videotaped, the outcome would not have been any different. Historically, the judges presiding over the criminal court in the city of Alexandria had never given anyone a suspended imposition sentence (SIS) prior to my plea to receive one. An SIS is when a defendant's offence is recognized as such, but the defendant is given probation for an extended period of time along with community service. During this period of time, if the defendant does not commit an unlawful act, displays remorse for their conduct, and completes the assigned community service, the offence is void and the defendant is given a second chance and fresh start.

Unfortunately, legislators have influenced judges throughout the Commonwealth of Virginia. Therefore, if they gave any defendant a SIS the issue would be discussed when they are up for reappointment to the bench. In other words, if such an issue were to be present during their reappointment period, the chance a judge will be reappointed is slim to none. Knowing this, people most familiar with my case believe Judge Kibbler made a business decision and not a moral one in regards to my sentencing.

I am aware our criminal justice system is a

multimillion-dollar business, and is driven by convictions, which dictate the amount of money generated. America is a capitalist society and failure is big business. It is estimated that over seven thousand high school students drop out of school every day in America. Our crime rate is constantly increasing, which creates a valid argument that more police officers, judges, social workers, and prisons are necessary.

There is certainly a need to keep our streets clean and safe, but it is imperative that we invest

> Make your mess your message...
>
> - Robin Roberts

more in education and resources that fuel intellectual capital. A 20 percent increase in college enrolment or a 10 percent decrease in crime nationally is priceless. It is nearly impossible to quantify the impact made when a parent is watching their child graduate from high school, or go off to college or get their first job. I think there is a strong argument to be made that the greater the reduction in juvenile delinquency, the greater the graduation rate.

For years, several of my friends ridiculed me for investing my time and intellectual capital in the transformation of communities. They believe that most communities cannot be improved, and that I should use my talent and energy to make a lot of money, paying off my student loans and living the American dream.

Despite what I have had to endure, my focus is on helping people change the world. I will continue to help change the world, serve God, and make an unmatched contribution to society regardless of what my external or internal circumstance may be at any given moment.

SIX

Never Give up Because Hard Work Does Pay Off

On March 8, 2012, I walked out of court after a long trial that changed my life forever. A few weeks later on May 4, 2012, I walked on stage to receive the prestigious Top 100 MBE® award. I was recognized among the group of outstanding women and minority entrepreneurs that fuelled this nation's economy through innovation, sacrifices, and dedication. It was a very kind gesture. I was picked from among

> To reach unparalleled success one must learn to lose money, in order to make a future decision unencumbered by the fear of loss.
>
> - Doug G. Vass

thousands of nominees as one of the "best and brightest" for my tireless work using education and technology to transform the lives of youth in the community and across the country, specifically through the Power Texting Mentor Network and Youth Town Hall events.

The award was presented on behalf of the Center for Business Inclusion and Diversity, Inc., greiBO media, Southwest Airlines, State Farm, UMUC and the State of

Maryland. During this ceremony Douglas F. Gansler, Attorney General for the State of Maryland, and Stephanie Blake, Mayor of the city of Baltimore, honored me for my leadership in the business community.

Later that month, on May 21, 2012, I accepted the Celebrating Partnership award at the joint award ceremony of Fairfax County and Fairfax County Public Schools, which honored the contributions of business and community partners for their innovative, problem-solving approaches. The event also recognized the new partnership between the BEM Foundation and Bryant High School (Bryant nominated me for this recognition). The attorney that prosecuted me was aware of the work and impact that I was making in Alexandria, Virginia, and across the country; nevertheless, I was pursued like I was anti-police with a history of criminal activity.

I could have given up, and I wanted to, but my hunger refused to let me. As I've mentioned before, I was leaning toward committing suicide at my lowest point. I mentioned a few things I did to keep myself inspired, but another thing I did was read motivational tips to help give me a winning edge. PickTheBrain (a link can be found on the resources page) is one of the many resources that I used to help fuel my passion and to further educate myself.

Below is a list of tips that I personally found inspiring and useful:

1- As Long as You Are Alive, Anything Is Possible: The only valid excuse you have to give up is if you are dead. As long as you are alive (and healthy and free), you have the choice to keep trying until you finally succeed.

2- Be Realistic: The chance of mastering something the first time you do it is almost non-existent. Everything takes time to learn and you will make mistakes. Learn from them.

3- Michael Jordan: Arguably the best basketball player of all time attributes his success to all his failures. He never gave up, even though he had missed thousands of shots, even missing the winning shot of the game many times. Every time he got knocked down, he got back up again.

4- Muhammad Ali: "Float like a butterfly, sting like a bee." Muhammad Ali is one of the best boxers the world has ever known. He suffered only five losses while having fifty-six wins. He was the first boxer to win the lineal heavyweight championship three times. This is a guy who literally knows how to get knocked down and get back up.

5- The Man Who Created the Marathon: Very long ago, an Athenian herald was sent to Sparta to get help when the Persians landed in Greece. It was said that he ran 240km in two days and after that he ran 40km to announce the victory of the Greeks, only to collapse and die on the spot from exhaustion. If you ever feel like things are difficult, imagine what it would be like to run 240km in two days. (Don't try this because it might kill you, but use it as an inspiration).

6- Chris Gardner and *The Pursuit of Happiness*: Have you seen the movie *The Pursuit of Happiness*? It is based on the life story of Chris Gardener, a man who went from the lowest of the lows, in an environment where most people would give up (no money, no job), to the highest of the highs (A millionaire with his own investment firm). If you ever think about giving up, watch this movie!

7- Kanye West: I'm pretty sure you have heard of the rapper Kanye West. Read his story. He is a big inspiration for many and proves that you can go from having very little to being among the most famous and respected people in the world.

8- Nelson Mandela: Campaigned for justice and freedom in South Africa. He spent twenty years in jail for his opposition to apartheid. Upon his release, he healed the wounds of apartheid by his magnanimous attitude toward his former political enemies.

9- You Are Strong: You are stronger than you think. One little setback is not enough to stop you from achieving your goals. Neither are 10 or 100 or 1000.

10- Prove Yourself: You don't want to be known as someone that is weak and gives up. Go out there and prove yourself to the world and to yourself. You CAN and WILL achieve what you set out to do. The only time you fail is when you give up.

11- Has It Been Done Before: If someone else can do it, you can do it. Even if it is only one other person in the world that has achieved what you have set out to achieve, that should be reason enough for you to never give up.

12- Believe In Your Dreams: Don't sell yourself short. In life, there are going to be tons of people who will try to bring you down and tell you what you want to achieve is not possible. Don't let anyone destroy your dreams.

13- Your Family and Friends: Let the people you love and who mean the world to you be your inspiration to persist and persevere. Maybe you need to try a different angle, study more or practice more, but don't give up!

14- You Are So Close: Often when you feel like you want to give up and you are about to give up, you are so close to making a huge breakthrough. Seth Godin has written an awesome book about this called *The Dip*. It's a riveting read that teaches that at any given time you are always just a heartbeat away from success.

15- There Are People Worse-Off: Right now, there are many people who are in a worse situation and environment than you are right now. Are you thinking about giving up on running five miles a week? Think about the people who are unable to even walk and how much they would give to be able to run five miles every day.

16- Improve Our World: When you achieve whatever you set out to achieve you can use your success to make a difference in the world or other peoples' lives.

17- Get Rich or Die Trying: Like 50 Cent says, "Get rich or die trying." 50 Cent is rich. He made it (although he did get shot nine times). Face your fears and don't take the easy way out by giving up.

18- Let the Haters Hate: There will always be haters. There will always be plenty of naysayers and people who try to tear you down. Don't pay attention to them, and don't take what they say to heart. Let the haters hate, and you keep believing in yourself.

19- You Deserve to Be Happy: Don't ever let anybody tell you otherwise. You deserve to be happy and you deserve to have success. Keep that mind set and never give up until you reach your destination!

20- Inspire Others: Be an inspiration to others by refusing to give up. Who knows what someone else can achieve because you never gave up and in turn inspired them not to give up.

21- Because I Tell You To: Not that I am any sort of guru or Godly figure, but if you want to give up, then don't, just because I'm telling you not to.

Throughout my life, I have read several quotes from some amazing people. I believe that you are what you eat, so I try to maintain a positive outlook and combat negative energy. I try to read a positive quote every day. There are millions of quotes, but here are a couple that have helped me overcome obstacles:

"The fact that you are "here" is a proof that you will get "there." The difference between "here" & "there" is "T" which is time. So don't give up!" - Olanrewaju Kazeem

"Life is positively forward. Although we do not always get what we want, it's when the going gets tough that we should never give up! Stay positive and stay with your dreams." - Author Unknown

Another thing that helped keep me inspired was hope. I always preached of providing hope for other people, and when the shadows of life shielded my eyes, hope was one of the few things that I could grab on to. In addition to hope, well, more like interweaved with the hope, was my reliance on faith to get me through the tough times. I got mad at God, fought with myself, prayed countless hours and read the Bible a lot, and in the end I knew that he had a plan for my life. The things that happened were meant to happen. I asked the question, "Why me?" a lot, but my thinking evolved into "Why not me?" Eventually I begin to thank God for the experience. Prayer has been powerful in my life. We can only do so much as humans, so I let the supernatural come into play. I believe in faith and God, and I consider myself a Christian. We can do everything imaginable, but in my humble opinion, faith is the most important ingredient to success. Faith and hope are the only things that I was able to hold on to even when the difficulties of life had shaken me something fierce. They are the great equalizers and they have certainly gotten me through my darkest hours.

Many have asked where my God was when I went through the trials and how he could let all of that (and my entire life) happen. All I know is that His will is going to happen, no matter how strong my volition is. You can look at a person's life and wonder why, but until they die, it isn't over for them. I'm still breathing, so the difficulties that I endure are simply the flames it takes to burn off all the doubt and weakness I may still possess. Victory comes to the one who can endure to the end.

Woodlawn reunion

Approximately three months after my trial, I flew to Chicago to visit my old community and elementary school. I was asked to be the keynote speaker and master of ceremony for an all-class reunion for James Wadsworth elementary school. It was a great opportunity to embrace my past life and celebrate the legacy of my school.

My elementary school was named after James Wadsworth, and when I attended the school I read about his story, and it made a profound impact on my life. Wadsworth was born to wealthy parents in Geneseo, in Livingston County in western New York. His father, James Wadsworth, was the owner of one of the largest portfolios of cultivated land in the state, and young Wadsworth was groomed to fulfil the responsibilities he would inherit. He attended both Harvard University and Yale University, studied law and was admitted to the bar, but had no intention of practicing. He spent the majority of his life managing his family's estate. Wadsworth built Hartford House in Geneseo, NY, upon his marriage in 1834 to the former Mary Craig Wharton of Philadelphia. Out of a sense of *noblesse oblige*, he became a philanthropist and entered politics, first as a Democrat, but then as one of the a organizers of the Free Soil Party, which joined the Republican Party in 1856. In 1861 he was a member of the Washington peace conference, an unofficial gathering of Northern and Southern moderates who attempted to avert war. But after war became inevitable, he considered it his duty to volunteer.

Unlike James Wadsworth, I was born into poverty. I too considered it my duty to volunteer my time and effort to make an impact on the world, attain a quality education, enter politics and become a philanthropist. James Wadsworth's story inspired me when I was a youth, and I marvel at how amazing the impact reading a simple story can make on your life as a child. I was honored and humbled to participate in an event honoring James

Wadsworth, the students that attended the school and the community.

Although Wadsworth was located in a drug-infested area, it had thousands of youth and was considered to be a landmark within the community. It has been through numerous transitions, both good and bad.

Hundreds of students attend the all-class reunion along with several educators, administrators and politicians. I sat down and spoke with my second-grade teacher Mrs. Kimbro, third-grade teacher Mrs. Ireland and sixth-grade teacher Mr. Pruitt. It was an awesome experience, and they all remembered me out of the hundreds of students they've taught.

The event opened up with a tremendous Gospel celebration led by alumni, and numerous speeches and awards followed it. I was one of the keynote speakers. Ms. Ursula Stevenson and I were both presented with James Wadsworth memorabilia from Mr. Housely Harville Jr. as a token of appreciation for our participation and commitment to excellence. Additionally, several alumni's children displayed their talents. One notable performance was by Brenda Nelson's, a childhood friend, daughter, who sang and brought the audience to their feet.

I was afforded the opportunity to perform with other childhood friends like Martin Johnson: a well-respected father of four, entrepreneur and former member of a rival breakdance group known as Tron; Ronald Bell: a husband, father of three, pastor, community advocate and professional counsellor; Darryl Moore: a father, husband and executive chef (Ron and Darryl are original members of the Star Blazers breakdance group); and, Dr. Devon Verse: another childhood friend (and original Star Blazer), successful entrepreneur and community activist.

We had not performed together in over twenty five years, so we didn't breakdance, settling for a little pop locking instead. It was an electrifying moment that I will never forget. It brought the crowd to their feet and rekindled old memories.

During the event, a song titled *Children Hold on to Your Dreams*, by William "Wee Gee" Howard, began to play and the entire audience sang aloud, paying homage to the school and community. This tune was the unofficial school song for us. It gave kids hope, an avenue to express themselves and an outlet to dream big. I can't explain how grateful I am for my experience at Wadsworth. It allowed me to spend some quality time with my family, friends and reunite with people I respect and admire.

The desire to remain the same v. the risk to evolve

The time came when the desire to remain the same became a greater risk than the will to evolve. My mother once said that it is easy to do nothing, but it takes an effort to do something. The hardest thing to do is try, but when I decided to put forth the time and energy to purse something positive, then I would change my circumstances, situations and destiny.

When everyone else is giving up, it makes you desire to stay the same so that you don't fail, but you have to risk evolution, you have got to be hungry to succeed. To some people, change is to make the form, nature, content, or future course of something different from what it is or from what it would be if left alone. Examples include changing

> **The time came when the desire to remain the same became a greater risk than the will to evolve...**
> **- Ron Mitchell**

one's name, opinion or the course of history. There are several ways to define the word change, but to become the epitome of it is a different thing.

As a youth I struggled with change. I became accustomed to an improvised community and I felt comfortable with my surroundings. I didn't know how different my community was until I began to travel across America and the world. Life has taught me that the road seldom traveled is lonely but not empty. Although I have made several mistakes and failed repeatedly throughout my life, I am grateful that my life has been an incentive for change.

The risk to evolve:

The risk to evolve is full of possibilities and uncertainty, but it can be rewarding. It will take courage, patience and a positive mental diet to combat the constant negative energy we are confronted with every day.

The Possibility of Today is one of the many resources that I personally find helpful. Here are some words of wisdom by Sibyl Chavis that I believe will help you maintain a positive diet:

"Have you ever thought about something you really wanted to try and accomplish, but then you changed? You somehow managed to talk yourself out of it or thought to yourself that now just was not the ideal time to pursue it." - Sibyl Chavis

In my life, the desire to stay the same became more

of a risk than evolving, and the idea of remaining stagnant in the horribly risky situations I was in became far too impossible in my mind than having the willpower to change. It was dangerous for me to stay the same, and the risk to evolve was high, but well worth it because it changed my life.

"Life is filled with opportunities and potential. That is one of the greatest things it offers to each and every one of us. I believe that everything is ours for the taking. However, in order for us to really take advantage of all we are capable of and all that life has to offer, we have to take some chances. We have to take some risks.

Often times we can get caught up with trying to organize and arrange the details of our life before we are willing to take a risk. We want things to be certain, and the timing to be just right in our minds, before we decide to transform our lives. It feels safer to be risk averse and we feel more responsible if we don't take chances on things until we have 100% assurance they will work out the way we envision." - Sibyl Chavis.

Is that how we really should be living?

The possibility of Today:

It is possible to be too apprehensive and as a result end up holding yourself back from what you can accomplish. You can overdo it by being too afraid of risk, subsequently missing out on some really quality opportunities that would have worked out in your best interest.

Of course, it is important to think things through and make certain you are as prepared as possible. At all times you have to give things an adequate amount of thought, and set things up in your life appropriately, but you can't buy into the belief that unless everything is perfectly planned out, the timing is impeccable and things are falling into place just as you would like, that you shouldn't move forward and pursue what you want.

"Never put your dreams on hold. Embrace the future and go for it. That doesn't mean you have to immediately change everything in your life and run blindly after your dreams. Perhaps your next best step is to research what you want and figure out your best course of action, or maybe you have reached a point where it is time to take the next step and make some changes.

Whatever the case may be, the most important thing is that in one way or another you are moving forward and in the direction of pursuing what you really want. Everything doesn't have to be certain before you do that. "In the majority of instances, when we are able to create the best opportunities, many things are uncertain." - Sibyl Chavis

"We may mistakenly think we are supposed to live our life according to a detailed plan, but, it really is okay to not know. In fact, it is ideal because once you let go a little of trying to control everything and you take some chances, that is when your wisdom and creativity can really take over and guide your life." - Sibyl Chavis

This good old truism should always be on the top of your mind: "There is wisdom in uncertainty."

"I think one of the best things we can do for ourselves is to open our heart and our mind to the absolute reality that we can have what we want. We can pursue our dreams and they will come to fruition. It is time to reassign any notions of fear or any other limiting beliefs that may be holding you back." - Sibyl Chavis.

Giving birth to possibilities

My life is dedicated to innovation and change. If we can change and improve the learning process then we can have a greater impact on human behavior, which I believe will help better develop our communities, fuel intellectual capital and provide solutions for issues affecting our neighborhoods.

The world is changing. As a result, the manner in which students learn today is in dire need of surgery. We can no longer ignore the needs of an evolving educational system. When I attended elementary school, books were the only manner in which a student received information and learned how to read and write. Today, several students use similar books filled with hundreds of words and a few pictures. The evolution of technology in the classroom is causing hardcover books to be used sparingly. Different from the traditional book, technology

> **Live for today and make it better than yesterday because tomorrow is not promised...**
>
> **–Ron Mitchell**

provides users with information presented in a more engaging, exciting and interesting manner with the click of a mouse or the tap of a finger. I believe e-learning will become the cornerstone for all classroom instruction, revolutionizing education as we know it today. If you desire to give birth to possibilities please consider the follow message. "Life is tough, that's a given. When you stand up you will be shoved back down. When you are down, you are going to be stepped on. My advice to you doesn't come with a lot of bells and whistles. It's no secret, you will fall down, you will stumble, you will get pushed, you will land square on your face. But every time that happens, you get back on your feet. You get up just as fast as you can, no matter how many times you need to do it. Remember this--success has been and continues to be defined as getting up one more time than you've been knocked down.

If experience has taught me anything, it's that nothing is free and living ain't easy. Life is hard, real hard, incredibly hard. You fail more often than you win, nobody is handing you anything. It's up to you to puff up your chest, stretch your neck and overcome all that is difficult, the nasty, the mean, the unfair. You want more than you have now? PROVE IT!

You want to be the very best there is, get out there and earn it!

Once you decide that, you will know where it is you

want to be and you won't stop pushing forward until you get there. That is how winners are made, at the end of the day success is what we all want, we all want to win, and the race will be won, there is no question about that. So come on, get out on top, run faster, dream bigger, live better than you ever have before. This is in you, you can do this, do it for yourself, prove it to yourself." - Gary Raser

---

SEVEN

My Greatest Success Is My Book of Failure

How I failed to use my gift of influence to prevent many of my peers from falling prey to the streets

My greatest successes in life are my failures. My experiences and interest in helping to change the world have inspired me to give birth to ideas and start several organizations. I have pursued many endeavours throughout my career. I have lost hope, money, relationships, friends and confidants. On many occasions, I have been trusted to lead people and make important decisions, and I have failed with both. Failure has been one of the constants in my life, and that is why I have and will continue to succeed. I owe a great debt to my community because it was a catalyst for change and gave me the desire to be an example for others. One of my childhood friends, Martin Johnson, once said, "In the going through there is a breakthrough."

Considering the following statistics made me believe that it was okay to be different, okay to lead and not follow others, okay to give and not take. In the 1990 census, Woodlawn had approximately 27,000 individuals, living in 10,000 households. Over 98% of the population was African American, over half were on some form of public aid, and the median household income was a little over $13,000 (when I was growing up). As of 2008, according to city-data.com, the median household income was just over $25,000, and in parts of eastern Woodlawn the white population was almost 30% and growing (fuelled by gentrification).

This data is merely a small insight as to one of the most notorious and violent communities in America. I was exposed to things that most teenagers and young adults learn about on the internet or in movie theatres.

According to Paul Street of the Chicago Urban League, the Illinois prison population has grown by more than sixty percent since 1990. That growth has been fuelled especially by Black admissions, including a rising number of nonviolent drug offenders. Two thirds of the state's more than 44,000 prisoners are African American. According to the Chicago Reporter, a monthly magazine that covers race and poverty issues, one in five Black Cook County (which contains Chicago and some of its suburbs) men in their 20s are either in prison or jail or on parole. For Cook County, Whites of the same gender and age possess the corresponding ratio of 1 in 104. Illinois has 115,746 more persons enrolled in its four year public universities than in its prisons. When it comes to Blacks, however, it has 10,000 more prisoners. For every African American enrolled in those universities, two and a-half Blacks are in prison or on parole in Illinois.

There were plenty of incidents when I could have used my influence to change the outcome of a situation; however, I didn't. I was young, scared or worried about what others would think of me. On some occasions, I was fearless and confronted the problem head on like a bull. Unfortunately, that approach is not always the wisest choice, and on more than one account my life was endangered.

One night, I decided to hang out with a few friends and go clubbing in Chicago. We were all break-dancers and enjoyed visiting clubs to battle against the best in the city. Sometimes during the heat of competition, people made offensive statements to help themselves gain an edge. Typically, during this type of event, we created a small circle on the dance floor, and we matched each other step for step doing innovative moves. All throughout the night we battled for applauses from the crowd. As the music got louder, we got more excited and began to do moves with the speed of light. A fellow dancer name Fanon did several breath-taking moves and concluded with a backspin. The crowd went crazy as the lights began to blink and move in sync with the beat. The disc jockey began to yell out our names, and the crowd got louder.

After a rival dancer did a number of moves I began to do several windmills, and then I did a head spin. While I was spinning on my head, someone kicked at me, which was very dangerous and could have caused a serious injury. Shortly after the kick, I heard a few members of my crew make threatening statements.

Immediately, I begin to spin on my back and slow down, getting up off the floor as a member of the rival crew began to throw punches at us. I took a few steps backward to get my composure and tried to calm down my crew. Hotheads prevailed and people started fighting, but my crew gathered our jackets and ran outside. I suggested that we all stay together and run to a local McDonald's to grab something to eat and defuse the situation. We all went, except for our buddy Nate, who insisted that he go back to his car. I knew that he was under the influence of some type of narcotic, but I didn't say anything and I watched him go.

The next day, I found out that the guys from the club had shot out the windows in his car, robbed him, and beat him up. Nate nearly died. This incident has haunted me for years. In the moment I knew that his life was at stake if he went back alone to his car. I had a great influence on Nate and should have taken his keys and forced him to come with us for protection. I was always taught to travel in bunches whenever in an unfamiliar neighborhood in Chicago. I failed Nate, his parents and other members of the crew. As a result, I became a more vocal and assertive person. I stopped worrying about what people thought about me and decided that I was no longer going to be selfish. From that moment on, I tried to make decisions that were in the best interest of others. Although I failed, I recognized that it was okay to fail. I am not perfect. I decided to stop being so hard on myself and start creating what would truly be possible in life by stretching myself to the limit. I began to take more risks and to surround myself with positive people. I started believing that I could raise the bar for myself and commit to goals that I once deemed unattainable.

Growing up in a drug-infested community can be depressing and uninspiring, but I had to find a way to keep myself motivated. The more I became focused, the harder I worked and the more I began to hear negative comments from the people around me. I began to detoxify them from my life, which helped me challenge myself and put my fear of failure to rest. I begin to remove certain words from my vocabulary. Works like cannot, will not, shall not, have not, could not and would not. And to stay inspired I also started making "no" react like diet soda and Mentos in my mouth.

How I was unable to provide a better life for my mother

One day after eating dinner, I sat by my grandmother and held her hand and began to play with her hair. It was like playing with a batch of grey cotton candy. I began to reminisce on several conversations we had throughout my life. She once likened my mother's having me as a son to winning the lottery. She asked me for my secret to working hard and keeping out of trouble in a gang and drug-infested community without being constantly prompted by any one particularly-supportive character. I thought about her question and wondered where my discipline originated. Eventually, I realized that my good character was not a gift that I had laid at my mother's feet, but a gift she had laid at mine. I remembered that my mother had shared with me the story of her arduous journey to Chicago in pursuit of a better life.

When I expressed this to my grandmother she began to smile. She said that my mother made many scarifies to provide a decent life for me and my brother and sisters. She said that my mother didn't shed tears externally because she was too proud, but she cried internally many nights. She said the tears symbolized the love and support that fell onto her children. Typically, parents expected no love or support in return. The children's love and support were reserved for their posterity. Being able to escape the harsh realities of the streets in Chicago affords me the prospect of bestowing my children with a better life than my own. I hope to mirror

> **Find something good within your life and give every ounce of positivity you have towards it, then watch how your life changes...**
>
> **- Author Unknown**

my mother's efforts. Her sacrifices are fundamental to my identity as a man and I owe her a great debt.

Despite her pain over my father's wilful estrangement from me and my brother, my mother showed me affection in her own way and concern. She worked long hours and struggled with our limited time together to teach me everything from the alphabet to respect for elders and peers.

During a conversation one day, she made it clear that she did not expect me to become wealthy or famous. She would mark herself a successful mother if her children lived an enjoyable life without the hardship she had to endure. Her genuine devotion moved me, and I loved her tremendously. I admire and miss her so much.

My mother's sacrifice would not come to fruition so easily. With neither a college education nor a wealthy family, my mother was forced to support her family through countless hours as a minimum-wage cashier. She reminded me that she had never expected me to become any type of professional, nor had she ever demanded that I achieve any particular grade in school. She simply prayed that at the very least I would one day graduate from high school and lead a more comfortable existence than she had. She hoped that raising my siblings in Chicago would help her realize a vision.

My mother was very tough on me, and she feared that I would follow in her footsteps. She feared that I would live a life of struggle, working several jobs to feed myself and my family, unsure of where my next meal would come from. She prayed that I would do well enough to command respect or at least have self-confidence.

Quite often, she endowed me with her own concept of Americanism, one in which hard work might allow me to rise above my background. Her sentiments inspired me, and I even promised her that I would make sure she did not have to work one day. When I made that statement my life began to change. I began to focus on building wealth and pursuing the same objectives as everyone around me. However, I refused to indulge in the same sort of illegal employment espoused by many of my friends. My professional goals bear a fundamentally different purpose—to vindicate my mother's sacrifices.

I worked hard for years. I wanted to be in a position to change my mother's situation. I believed I could someday bring greater meaning to her years of misfortune. I often prayed that one day I could proudly say to her, "Mother, your life has not been wasted. Your efforts and sacrifices have brought me into the world and instilled in me values that make me a hard-working, family man. I am leading a great life."

Aside from my employment changes and new goals, I also began to treat her differently. Simple things like tone, smiles or touching her hand drastically softened the shell she had developed. I treated her like she was bigger than life, and to me she was.

An elderly woman in my neighborhood, Ms. Okeef, once told me that I was fortunate because, "There are two different types of parents: parents who live for themselves and parents who live for their children."

A parent of the latter type, my grandmother raised her daughter to value the lives and happiness of her children above her own. My grandmother said that she regularly felt the pain of my mother's struggles and earnestly wished to see her out of her harsh circumstances. I now acknowledge that through her countless efforts to raise her children as a Black woman, my mother granted me a free education, the liberty and support to choose the person I want to become, the opportunity to care for my own family and the ability to repay her sacrifices.

During our chat my grandmother's eyes started to water so I kissed her forehead. Although my mother and grandmother are both dead now, and I failed to provide her with the comfort and happiness she has given me, I refuse to give up until I use my mother's gifts to blaze a trail for those that will one day follow in my footsteps.

EIGHT

Stay Hungry and Stay Humble

To be hungry is to be humble. In the movie *Forrest Gump*, Tom Hanks played a character named Forrest Gump. In one famous scene a woman walked up and sat down beside him on the bench. He introduced himself and offered her some chocolate before reciting the famous words, "My momma always said, 'Life was like a box of chocolates. You never know what you're gonna get.'" I agree with Forrest's mother. No one can predict the future. Every day is a new beginning and an opportunity to live and experience the unknown. The unknown can be a good or a bad experience, depending on your attitude about the situation.

Some experiences force us to become more humble and grateful for the things we often take for granted like food, shelter, life and good health. Illness is one of the negative aspects of the unknown, but still an area we should all remain humble. Steve Jobs, the former CEO of Apple Incorporated, oversaw the development of iTunes, iPods, iPhones, and iPads. On the services side, he watched over the company's retail stores, the iTunes Store and the

App Store. The success of these products and services provided several years of stable financial returns, and propelled Apple toward becoming the world's most valuable publicly traded company in 2011. Though they weren't always successful, their reincarnation is regarded as one of the greatest turnarounds in business history.

Unfortunately, in 2003 Jobs was diagnosed with a pancreas neuroendocrine tumor. Though it was initially treated, he reported a hormone imbalance and underwent a liver transplant in 2009. He went on medical leave for most of 2011, resigned in August that year, and was elected Chairman of the Board. He died of respiratory arrest related to his metastatic tumor on October 5, 2011. Despite the impact that he made on the world through technology, and his many achievements, I am sure he never envisioned becoming ill at the peak of his career.

Steve Jobs has inspired many around the world, including myself, and has made an unmatched contribution to the global society. He has confirmed that no one is exempt from pain, sickness or poor health. I truly believe life is a journey, and you never know when it will end. I try to embrace each moment with this in mind. I have now embraced humility although it is difficult to do at times, especially when people are reminding you that you are beautiful, perfect or the best in every way imaginable (not that people say that about me).

Society encourages competition and individuality. Yet humility still remains an important virtue. Today, humility is considered vital in most spiritual traditions, and outside the traditions it is an authoritative tool. It can help you develop more fully, enjoy richer relationships with others and grow as person. To be humble *is* to be hungry. During the journey toward your goals, you will likely be knocked down, offended, ridiculed and told that you can't accomplish your dreams. Embrace this type of experience in order to humble yourself, but also cull it to fortify your hunger.

To combat several comments, awards, gestures and other things that may cause me not to be humble, I constantly search for tips to encourage humility. Here are a few tips I gathered from WikiHow.com that I believe you may find helpful:

1. Understand your limitations. No matter how talented you are, there is almost always somebody who can do something better than you. Look to those who are better and consider the potential for improvement. Even if you are the best in the world at doing one thing, there are always

other things that you cannot do, and may never be able to do. Recognizing your limitations does not mean abandoning your dreams, and it does not mean giving up on learning new things or improving your existing abilities.

2. Recognize your own faults. We judge others because it's a lot easier than looking at ourselves. Unfortunately, it's also completely unproductive and, in many cases, harmful. Judging others causes strife in relationships, and it prevents new relationships from forming. Perhaps even worse, it prevents us from trying to improve ourselves. We make judgments about others all the time, usually without even realizing it. As a practical exercise, try to catch yourself in the act of judging another person or group of people, and whenever you do, judge yourself instead. Consider how you can improve yourself.

3. Count your blessings. Much of what we give ourselves credit for is actually a product of luck. Suppose you graduate from an Ivy League university at the top of your class. You definitely deserve a lot of credit for the many hours of studying and for your perseverance. Consider, though, that there is someone just as bright and hardworking as you who had less supportive parents, grew up in a different place, or just had the bad luck to make one wrong choice in life. You could be in their position instead.

Always remember that with a little bad luck yesterday, your whole life could be different today; furthermore, today could be the day your luck changes.

4. Appreciate the talents and qualities of others. Challenge yourself to look at others and appreciate the things they can do, and, more generally, to appreciate people for who they are. Understand that everybody is different and relish the chance you have to experience different people. You will still have your personal tastes, your likes and dislikes, but train yourself to separate your opinions from your fears and you will appreciate others more. I.e., you will be humbler.

5. Stop comparing. It's nearly impossible to be humble when we're striving to be the "best" or trying to be better than others. Instead, try describing things more objectively. Rather than saying that so and so is the best guitarist ever, say what exactly it is that you appreciate about his skills, or simply say that you like his playing style. Let go of meaningless, simplistic comparisons, and you'll be able to enjoy doing things without worrying about whether you're better or worse at said things than others.

6. Don't be afraid to make mistakes. Part of being humble is understanding that you will make mistakes. Understand this, and understand that everyone else makes mistakes, and

you will have a heavy burden lifted off of you. Any one person can know only the smallest bits and pieces of the tremendous knowledge that has accumulated over the past. What's more, each person experiences only a sliver of the present, and knows little to nothing of the future.

7. Don't be afraid to defer to others' judgment. It's easy to acknowledge that you make mistakes and that you're not always right. Somewhat more difficult, however, is the ability to acknowledge that in many cases other people — even people who disagree with you — may be right. Deferring to your spouse's wishes, to a law you don't agree with, or even, sometimes to your child's opinion takes your recognition of your limitations to a different level. Instead of simply saying that you know that you're fallible, you take action based on that fact. Of course, if you know that a particular course of action is wrong, you shouldn't follow it. On closer inspection though, you may realize that you don't actually know this as often as you think you do.

8. Rejuvenate your sense of wonder. Because we as individuals know practically nothing, you'd expect that we'd be awestruck more often than we typically are. Children have this sense of wonder, and it inspires the curiosity that makes them such keen observers and capable learners. Do you really know how your microwave works?

Could you build one on your own? What about your car? Your brain? A rose? The jaded, *I've seen it all* attitude makes us feel far more important than we are. Be amazed like a child and you will not only be humbled, you will also be readier to learn.

9. Seek guidance. Contemplate moral texts and proverbs about humility. Pray for it, meditate on it, do whatever it takes to get your attention off yourself. If you're not into spirituality, consider the scientific method. Science requires humility. It requires that you let go of your preconceived notions and judgments and understand that you don't know as much as you think you do.

10. Remain teachable. Find people you aspire to be like in certain areas, and ask them to mentor you. Under mentorship, good boundary setting, confidentiality and discernment are required. As soon as you cross the line of being *un-teachable* bring yourself back down to earth.

11. Help others. A big part of being humble is respecting others, and part of respecting others is helping them. Treat other people as equals and help them because it is the right thing to do. It's been said that when you can help others who cannot possibly help you in return, you have learned humility.

12. Practice gentleness. Gentleness of spirit is the sure path to humility. Use Aikido where possible when faced with conflict: absorb the venom from attacks and react with gentleness and respect.

13. Associate with and help out people in less-fortunate situations, especially the poor, weak, etc. Appreciate your talents. Being humble doesn't mean you can't feel good about yourself.

14. Self-esteem is not the same as pride. Both come from a recognition of your own talents and qualities, but pride, which leans toward arrogance, is rooted in insecurity about yourself. It is fine to talk about yourself a little, but make a conscious effort to ask people about themselves too. It's also a good idea to listen more when someone is talking or responding to you. Be kind and considerate. Help others and tell them you are there for them.

15. Think about the abilities you have, and be thankful for them. Keep in mind that being humble has many benefits. Humility can help you be more content with your life, and it can also help you endure bad times and improve your relationships with others.

Being humble is also essential to being an effective

learner. If you think you know it all then you won't be open minded enough to seek out new knowledge. Humility is also, somewhat counter-intuitively, an excellent tool for self-development in general. After all, if you feel superior, you have no incentive to improve. Most of all, being humble allows you to be honest with yourself. Never brag about what you have given to receive. Seek trusted and wise counsel and obtain accountability partners if you find this to be a weakness in your life. Pride comes before the fall, and prevention is definitely better than medication. Be loving and kind hearted at all times. You never know when someone might need to reach out to you.

NINE

What If

What if we became a color-blind society and America focused on educating and developing the brightest minds? Would we be a better nation? I believe we would. Racism and discrimination have prevented America from fulfilling its potential. Racism, like most -isms, develops from ignorance, assumption or poor education. No one is born hating another person based off the color of their skin, though developing minds that are saturated in an environment where hate is practiced, taught or demonstrated can certainly lead said mind to begin to hate.

An easy way to develop a hatred for someone is based off of previous experience. If a man walked down an alley at night and was robbed by two Black thugs, the victim would not be happy. If that same man was in a mall, and a Black lady cursed him out for stepping on his shoe, he would not be happy. If that same man was driving and suffered a collision at the fault of an intoxicated Black man, he would understandably not be happy. All of the above do not provide the victim with a reason to hate the race solely based off of race and experience. Beyond the obvious, the man was in bad situations, and it just so happened that he was assaulted and insulted by Blacks. That does NOT give him a reason to hate all Blacks. I'm suggesting that the nation begin to separate people from situations. Instead of jumping to the conclusion that Black people are bad because you have bumped heads with a few, understand that the situations were bad, and bad people affected your life. It should not matter that they were Black. One person will never represent an entire race appropriately.

Because racism is not grounded in accurate facts or findings, it's one of the harder things to eliminate. Racism is a description of an emotion felt, and emotions are one of the trickier human experiences to wilfully change. That being said, this does not mean racism can't stop, it means we have to make a conscious decision to stop it where we see it in our lives and the lives of those around us. Everyone could use a little more love. If there was no hate, love doesn't necessarily have to be the result, but the disappearance of hatred sure makes loving a whole lot easier.

What if you loved others the way you wanted to be loved? Would they love *you* the way you wanted to be loved? Love is impossible to measure, and since it can't be measured a value can never be placed on it. Love can be as small as holding someone's hand when they're crying, or as big as yanking a person from in front of oncoming traffic, but in either case the person experiencing the love is grateful. Try creating a love journal just to see how important love is in your life. Write down all the ways you feel loved. For me, I feel loved when someone I've helped gives me a hug, or shakes my hand and says thank you. After you understand some ways you feel loved, write down who normally gives you the love and when. The first day would be what's already happened, but every day after see how often someone shows a little love. Write it down and watch your list escalate. Feel free to add in additional ways you feel loved as your journal grows.

What if we didn't make a big deal about someone's social or economic status, and focused on developing mental talents? Would we be more advanced intellectually as a nation? I believe the more we invest in our nation's youth, the more it will improve our intellectual capital. Even the most hateful people in the country don't hate the country. If they did, they wouldn't stick around, or they would proactively engage in nationally-detrimental terrorism. They may dislike a policy or a law or a particular group of people, but overall they enjoy living here (or at least they enjoy the freedoms living here entails). With that in mind, even the most hateful people should work toward creating a more intelligent America. The more holistically successful America is, the more successful the citizens can be. Who cares if the person next to you doesn't have much money? If you answered, "I do," then you should be flogged. Money is not, and will not ever be, a valid mode of evaluating a human being's worth. If someone is poor, it does not mean that they are lower than you. If it did, money would be wired into our DNA, or it would have squeezed out our mothers during our birth. Last time I checked, we all escaped the womb with nothing but an umbilical cord. Everyone with money either received it as a hand out from someone else (like their parents, the government or a family situation), or they worked hard to make it happen (a job, an investment, etc.) (But if you think about it, working is still receiving money from someone else, so at the root money can only be given).

In a capitalistic society it's hard to remove the value of money from the humans that hold it, but we all need to view money in a different way. Money is a means to an end. It is not a person's definition. It is a way for that person to provide for their needs. It should also be a way to help others provide for their needs. If we invested the money we make back into the country, everyone wins.

If you're looking purely at the socio-economic status of a person in order to imagine yourself as superior, you are simply creating another dumb excuse to try and classify a person based off conditions that don't have a thing to do with the quality of that individual. So one person is a CEO and another is a garbage collector. Why does that inherently create a value? Even as you read that, you're thinking the CEO is better than the garbage collector, and that is what we need to change. Until you get to know individuals, you cannot and should not create a value for them (even then you shouldn't give them a value, but I don't want to delve too deep, so I'll leave that where it is). For all you know the CEO is a rapist and the garbage collector once saved 500 children from a school. Now who has more value in your mind (I really want to discuss why you still should not assign a value for the garbage man, who you undoubtedly started thinking was better than the rapist CEO, but that discussion is for the sequel)?

We need to change the way that we view value in human beings. We are special because of our personalities, our dedication, and our desires to be kind to others, not because of money or status. Those three qualities are based on opinion. A wonderful personality to me may not be the same for you. A dedicated person may mean someone who wakes up at five every morning to walk their dog, but it may also mean a person who goes to bed at five every morning so that they can finish the work they had tasked for the day. Since we are special because of things that are based on opinion, be extremely hesitant when associating value on another person. In the end, we should all keep ourselves meek and refuse to place a value on others, but if you must place value somewhere, place it on things like personality, dedication, and a desire to be kind to others.

What if there was no such thing as public or private school, and there was just one educational system? Could we find a solution for the toughest problems affecting society? Yes! If all the schools received the same amount and type of resources, then we could produce better students, ideas and solutions. I understand the difference between private and public, how government funding fuels one and parents/private givers fuel the other, but if we could formulate a way to give a quality education to everyone then the whole nation would thrive. Private schools were created for a couple of reasons, but the main reason was to teach a specific curriculum untouched by the government (by the way, private schools actually started before public schools, but I'm speaking of the modern private and public schools). I'm aware that there are parents that want their children to receive a religious-based (or other specified form like classical or military) education, but those aren't the situations I'm referring to. I'm referring to the times when parents pull their kids out of school because the schools weren't good enough, leaving behind the underprivileged kids to suffer through a shoddy educational process that maturates them in failure's harsh cocoon.

Children in America should never (ever, ever, ever!) be subjected to a poor education because their school is underfunded. Instead of funding the oil industry so that we can all pollute the planet some more, we need to fund the school system so the children can learn to create more effective alternative fuels. Or better yet, what if we funded the kids until they created a way to eliminate vehicles all together? Doesn't make sense in your mind? Well it doesn't make sense in my mind either, but that's my point, we haven't figured it out but maybe the children will.

That being said, education does not rest entirely on the shoulders of the school system and its employees. Education starts in the home, and parents have to step it up a few notches in order to initiate the child's hunger for learning.

In my opinion, the year our education system is revamped will be the year America's future takes a turn for the better. As long as a lack of money dictates how good an education is given, America will continue to produce a minimal amount of brilliance. My heart grows heavier the more I think about the kid who has the cure for cancer locked away in her brain. It sags down to my stomach, getting heavier and heavier as I imagine the key to her brain being dangled on a string of money that she'll never be able to reach.

What if we didn't have illegal drugs in America? Would there be fewer crimes committed? Yes, a lot of the crimes committed are drug related today and have turned many of our communities into ghettos. So think twice about selling that dime bag. It could not only ruin someone else's life, but it will ruin your life. Drugs are never the answer to anything aside from the how-can-I-get-into-jail question.

What if we inspired the best criminal minds to be the leading business minds? Would Microsoft or Apple or JPMorgan Chase have been established several years before their existence? I believe many companies could have been developed many years earlier. There are several gang leaders, thugs and drug kingpins that possess the identical intestinal fortitude and talents displayed by many of the world's most successful business leaders. Of course, they weren't presented with the same opportunities as others, and the decisions they made sent them down the wrong paths. So how do we fix that? It all starts with the education, but this goes beyond that. It reaches to the communities itself, to the availability of resources in the community. Most crime sprouts from necessity, so if we take away the lack of resources, many crimes would be eliminated. There will always be greedy individuals who are out to make the quickest buck, but there are enough criminals who do what they have to do to survive, and they are the ones who could be tomorrow's leaders if we afford them the opportunity.

What if there was no such thing as greed? Would we have access to some of the world's most innovative products? If you take the time to mull over the need for greed, you'll come up lacking. Greed is not simply wanting to obtain something, it's wanting an excess of what is necessary and hoarding what is received. I was once informed that a successful comedian had a collection of over 100 cars. Take that in for a few seconds. Just think of all the good he could be doing with the money that he's spent on 100 cars. That's probably one hundred small houses, or one million meals to fill children's stomachs, or one billion articles of clothing. And to think I thought having one car was a privilege.

What if all food was organic? Would there be less health issues in America? If the majority of the food consumed was organic and natural, I think it would decrease the amount of health-related issues because natural food is healthier. The more we play with what God has put on this earth, the less healthy it becomes. Since food is usually shipped from all over, and grown in ginormous quantities, the reason for much of the processing, growth hormones and pesticides is a need that is paired with cost efficiency. If it costs more to go through a field and kill each worm on a fruit, and it's cheaper to spray on preventative measures, the greedy get to spraying. No matter how much a company says it is concerned with the health of the consumer, their main priority is to make money. But if the only market was an organic market, or a market for minimally processed foods, the price on such items would go down and the access would go up. If you ask anyone why they don't buy organic they will say because it's more expensive.

The issue with fast food is simple. People visit fast food restaurants for their convenience. If they don't have time to cook, or if they're too lazy to cook, then they can order food out and not have to worry about it. That problem will only be solved when America slows down (primarily relating to work) and gets off the couch for a change.

Perhaps if we all promoted growing food at home again the nation would be a healthier place. Can you get a vegetable garden going in or around your house? If you're not sure, find out and reap the benefits of fresh, untampered with produce. Your body will thank you. Realistically, it will still take more than a few gardens to get healthy. It'll take commitment from food companies, dedication from consumers and desires from everyone to make the nation a healthier place.

What if law and medical schools (or any collegiate institutions for that manner) were more affordable? Would we have better physicians, lawyers and legislators? Yes. The cost of acquiring a medical and legal education has prevented some of the best and brightest from pursuing both fields as a career. If law school was free, there would be a lot more incentive to attend. Sure, there will be people that don't want to go, but there will also be the people that will go and will succeed. How many have wanted to do something but shied away from it because it promised to add hundreds of thousands of dollars of debt to life? How many kids grow up saying they want to be a doctor, but when faced with the decision opt not to attend medical school? Out of that number, at least half decide the monetary burden is too extensive to bear.

What if Barack Obama was not the first minority to become president of the United States of America, but the fourteenth? Would America be what it should be today? Can America really thrive when the interests of "everyone" is only enacted by people who have not seen every viewpoint? How can a person who has never known what it's like to grow up as a minority truly have a heart for the problems and passions of minorities? What if it was prohibited for a single race to enter into the white house for more than two separate terms? What if it was mandatory for a Latino, Black, or Asian (all of whom would be born in America, of course) citizen to become president before another white president was elected (same could go for income, or industry, or location, etc.)?

What if politicians had to undergo controlled experiences in the laws and bills they passed? For example, if a politician wanted to pass a law that created a higher tax on diapers, perhaps the politician should be put in the same position as the people who suffer from such a law. Perhaps if situations were simulated proportionately in the politician's life, then they would have more of a heart for the people in need because they would have experienced a small amount of the issues.

What if there was no light? Would there be darkness? Consider the process of elimination if you take light out of the equation darkness is the only thing remaining. That principle should be the guiding idea behind everything we do. If I don't create light for the world, who will? Someone has to bring a little light or we'll all be in darkness. You are the light of the world, and it's imperative that you let your light shine so that everyone can see it. Your light is your job, your education, your attitude, your hunger.

What if you didn't attend college? Would you likely become more successful? Statistics suggest that college graduates earn more money than those that have only completed high school. However, there are some exceptions. Bill Gates and several other entrepreneurs never completed college, but they studied their craft and spent countless hours developing their talent. You don't have to attend college to succeed. On the flip side of the coin, just because you attend college does not mean you will succeed. There are plenty of unemployed college graduates who have nothing to show for their degree except for mounds of debt. There are just as many high school graduates who work dead-end jobs since they aren't qualified for anything better.

What you need to understand is that success is not based on one thing. To be successful, you've got to be hungry, and you've got to pursue what you want. You are a cheetah and your goal is that juicy antelope trotting along like you aren't fast enough. Run until you get what you want and feast on the spoils of your hard work.

What if you didn't laugh often? Would you cry more? Laughter and crying are both from emotions triggered by an action or thought. In spite of the situation, it is up to you to determine the type of impact someone or something will have on you as a person. One of the most powerful tools you can use is the tool of happiness. Happy people live better lives. If you don't know what the difference between joy and happiness is, ask someone smarter than you and figure out a way to plant it down in your heart.

Laughter is a gift from God, and you should utilize it as much as possible. Was that situation really that bad? If it wasn't then laugh about it, learn from it and live enlightened. If it was that bad, then cry from it, learn from it, live enlightened and laugh about it later. You control your emotions, they don't control you.

What if you studied harder in school? Would you receive a scholarship? Most successful people believe that hard work does pay off and is a key ingredient used to achieve their goals. There's only one way to find out the answer to this. My answer is "yes." If you study hard, then you will reap a bountiful harvest. If I'm wrong, what did you lose?

What if you didn't give up so easily? Would you be more successful? There is no effort required to give up, but to succeed it will take willpower, motivation and dedication. I hesitate to use illustrations of other people because you are your own person, but Thomas Edison is said to have unsuccessfully created the light bulb over 1,000 times. If he had given up, we'd all be rubbing sticks together for fire. I pray that we never find out what society will lack if you give up.

What if you were adopted? Would you want to meet your biological parents? Some people have said they would like to know who their biological parents are, and others have decided that they didn't want to know. Remember tomorrow is not promised. How different do you think your life would be if you were adopted? Would your parents treat you better or worse than your siblings?

What if you knew the day your mother or father would die? Would you cherish every moment you spent together until then? Family is a very important asset to have, but unfortunately there are thousands of children living in foster homes. Be grateful for the family you do have. You never know when it will change.

Since we don't know when our parents' numbers will be called, live every day like it will be their last. No matter how rough you feel they are treating you, or how hurt you feel by them, they are still your parents. They are doing their best, and they are not perfect. They will fail in some areas and succeed in others, but it is your responsibility to make their life as easy as you can. Don't make the mistakes I made growing up, neglecting to appreciate my mother's role until it was too late. I challenge you to change how you talk, respond and act around your parents. If they don't start to treat you better as a result, shoot me an email (address in the back) with the pertinent information and I'll give them a call about it.

What if it was not your parents that were going to die, but you that only had one day to live? Would you live tomorrow like it was you last? Today could be your last day on earth. Tomorrow is not promised. Pursue your dreams and try to make a positive impact. This *does not* mean party every day and experience every sensation known to man. It *does* mean make the most of your current situation, learn from what you can and live like life matters.

What if you had cancer? Would you want to find a cure? Most people that have been diagnosed with cancer would do anything to find a cure. I'm convinced we have a cure for cancer, although we don't know where it is. The solution could be inside of you.

What if you had HIV and to find a cure you had to die? Would you be willing to die? In life you will have to make sacrifices, and although it may not be this type, a friend may need an organ replaced or blood donated, and you may be the one to give it. Would you help a friend live if it meant you would be short something valuable? Would you donate one of your eyes so that you *and* your friend could see? What about if it was your brother? Your mother? Your son?

What if you had one wish? What would it be? Would your wish help others or would it just help you? Why not go out and be your own genie? Who's to say that wish you just had can't come true? Who's to say you can't make that wish come true?

What if you could see into the future? Would you change the outcome of your life? If you would, you would likely be making a choice that would only benefit you and no one else. Stop and think of how much impact you've already had on the world at your age. On the right hand, that one word of encouragement you gave to a friend could be the motivation they needed to stay alive. On the left hand, those slurs you heaped on that person's head could be the last chink before their chain snaps and they commit suicide. Your current decisions may seem insignificant, but every ripple starts small.

What if finding a cure for cancer meant that you would have to sacrifice your life? Would you be willing to? Personally, I would be willing to sacrifice my life if it would change the world, but just because I would do something does not mean that you should. I have experienced the unimaginable and lived a very diverse life, so you would be missing out on a lot more. Yet and still, what would you sacrifice to get the results that are needed?

What if you gave your best in everything you tried. What if you always chased your dream and were never satisfied with average? What if you got hungry, stayed hungry, and changed the world? I don't know for sure, but let's live and find out.

TEN

Success Cannot Be Measured

Over the years I have been asked *what is success* and if it could be measured? Success can be defined as an achievement of something planned or attempted. It is important that you determine what success means to you. For you, being successful may include not only enjoying what you do, but also creating value for others. So in addition to spending time with your loved ones and enjoying your life, you also need a way to gauge whether or not you are actually creating value for other people.

> If there were no such thing as failure, then there would be no such thing as success...
>
> -Tom Langley

When we set goals in any area of our life, we need to determine beforehand what our intended result is and how we will recognize it when we arrive. Establishing ahead of time what success looks and feels like also gives us the opportunity to program our nervous system with the exact feelings that success will bring. This creates anticipation that, in turn, helps us to take consistent action in the direction of our goals. You decide exactly what it means to be successful in any area of your life. The time to make that decision is during the period you begin establishing your goals. Doing so will allow you to identify and celebrate each personal success along the way.

People measure success in many different ways and on many different levels. When setting goals in life it's important that we identify what success means to us personally. That way when we succeed we will know it. To me, success means completing a task, and, when looking back, thinking I couldn't have done it better. To succeed is to complete a task or assignment on time in an excellent manner, but that's only half of it. The results should be good and the people involved should gain a valuable lesson or experience. For example, if you are tasked with a group project, and only two out of four people really did the work, I wouldn't call that success. If everyone participated and worked together, providing a valuable, deliverable result then it is a success. So I think both the result and the process should be excellent to call something a success.

Depending upon the individual, success can also be an end result as well as a journey. The definition relies upon your personal mantras and values. You may value and measure success as seeing a goal and achieving, it or perhaps you measure it as smashing the goal out of the water. You may see success as a process of enlightenment or your way through life. Success can be small or big and, depending on your competitive nature, you may see a success in a small win. Then again, maybe that win is just a small step to what you consider success. Success for a single mother of five can be getting her children through college on a tiny budget. In other words, success is what you believe it is and whatever you make it.

ELEVEN

Make Extraordinary an Ordinary Day

To become hungry is to be extraordinary and not ordinary. The world is full of ordinary people and extraordinary problems. There is a great need for extraordinary people that are willing to take risks and change the world as we know it today. Extraordinary people have inspired and developed many ideas, products, tools, services, medicines and laws that have transformed the world. No one is born extraordinary. Therefore, ordinary people become extraordinary and do incredible things.

Every person with decisional capacity has the right to be ordinary and refuse to work hard or give up when faced with adversity, despite the impact it may have on others. That said, some people and groups believe that being ordinary is acceptable while others disagree. The latter argues that it is morally worse to be ordinary when the possibility for extraordinary is present. Their train of thought follows the idea that people have a general obligation to be the best they can be to sustain their own lives. A certain degree of adversity and hardship is involved. To ignore the basic minimum requirement, which is to put forth your best effort to sustain one's life, is morally wrong because it undermines life and the unlimited possibilities contained within.

There is a distinction between ordinary and extraordinary. What is ordinary for one person may be extraordinary for another. Still, ordinary and extraordinary characteristics are generally categorized as follows:

Extraordinary -

1. Innovative, experimental, unusual

2. High risk

3. Complex, relatively high tech

4. Time consuming, great effort required

5. Potential to have great benefits

6. Relatively expensive

7. Very few will seek to do it (may involve a great sacrifice)

8. Usually involves a lot of patience, pain or distress

Ordinary -

9. Low risk of harm

10. Routine

11. Simple, relatively little effort

12. Some benefits acquired

13. Relatively inexpensive

14. Most people can do it

15. Causes little pain or distress

Ordinary people do extraordinary things every day and are inspired to excel. Here are a few tips that can help you do extraordinary things:

o Follow your dreams. If you don't, then you will crush your dreams and one day stop dreaming altogether.

o You don't want to regret a failure to pursue your dreams or goals.

o Remember that you will regret tomorrow the things you were too scared to do today.

o Dreamers who took action have created many of the extraordinary things around you.

Following your dreams doesn't always turn out as planned, but neither does anything extraordinary. Do you want to be remembered? I do. Almost everybody does. People remember those who follow their dreams because they do extraordinary things. Unfortunately, everyone will not support your efforts and there will be haters. Use the negativity as fuel and keep doing what you do. Ordinary people inspire others to follow and live their dreams by giving an extraordinary effort. To be hungry is to be extraordinary.

Extraordinary people learn from their failures. Since you will fail on your path, you'll learn a lot too. Why limit yourself and be ordinary and do what everybody else is doing? Remember the ordinary people that put forth the extra effort, extra energy, extra passion and extra time are the ones who become extraordinary. Take a chance. Make extraordinary an ordinary day.

There are several resources that are vital to succeed. Resources like money, exposure and support to name a few. Some argue that each one can be replaced by another resource depending upon the circumstances. I agree; however, there is no substitute for hunger. It is the great equalizer. If you are hungry you will be willing to do the things today that others will not do to have the success they can only dream about tomorrow. To be hungry is to have no boundaries or limits, to look beyond words and see what others cannot, to maximize the moment and discover new possibilities. You've got to do what it takes to succeed.

No matter what.

ABOUT THE AUTHORS

Ron Mitchell is the founder of the BEM Foundation, a non-profit organization that works with "at-risk" youth from ages thirteen to nineteen. Its mission is to arm young adults with academic tools, resources, and leadership skills that will benefit their respective lives and community. Ronald is the creator of the BEM Methodology, a transformative tool designed to improve communities and change lives. BEM's motto is "make the unimaginable a reality."

In 2012, he was recognized as one of the TOP 100 Minority and Women Entrepreneurs in America for his enterprising entrepreneurship, which helped to fuel this nation's economy through innovation, sacrifice, and dedication. His willingness to overcome adversity and make significant contributions to organizations, communities across the globe, and change lives has inspired many. For the past decade, Ron Mitchell has served as an advisor to organizations, leaders, students, athletes, and professionals around the country. He is a recognized thought leader and change management expert for his innovative problem solving, leadership, negotiation talents, organizational strategy and inspirational peak performance. He has been honored consistently for his business acumen, strategic intellect and humanitarian endeavors. Ron has partnered with several Fortune 500 and nonprofit foundations to help transform communities and provide assistance to inner-city youth and senior citizens across America. Ron has directly impacted the lives of thousands of people from across the globe with his community service, public speaking engagements and live events. What began as a young person's desire to play professional sports, escape the drug-infested ghetto of Chicago, and become an advocate for humanity, for political and social economic injustice, has fueled a man to change the lives of many individuals and the world.

Jeremie Guy was born and raised in the Washington D.C. metro area. He is usually reading, writing or eating. If he can't be found typing away at his computer screen, he is undoubtedly hunting for the most bizarre food in your state. Tasked with trying every type of food at least once, he's always searching for a plethora of things to add to his palate. So whether it's Kangaroo in Kansas City, or Iguana in Virginia, if you present him with it he will try it. He graduated from Towson University with an English Degree in 2010, received an AFPA Personal Training certification in 2011, and a Louisiana State University Shreveport graduate certificate in nonprofit management in 2012. Always eager to learn something new, Jeremie is waiting for his next opportunity to achieve inspiration through education.

He has written and edited freelance for a number of organizations, and he ghostwrites part time. He has won first place in a handful of writing contests and his creative works have appeared in over twenty publications, including an appearance in Earthbound Fiction's short story anthology *DARK STARS*. He is also a member of Lambda Iota Tau, international literary honors society. He attributes all of his opportunity and success to God and his savior, Jesus Christ.

Resources

Commercial viewed in Best Buy -

http://www.youtube.com/watch?v=lJNT_y-a4Zc

The Possibility of Today – Simple tips for living today better than yesterday

http://www.possibilityoftoday.com/

Pick the Brain (motivational, productivity, health, and self-improvement website) –

http://www.pickthebrain.com

WikiHow – answers on how to do virtually anything –

http://www.wikihow.com

We would love to hear from you. Email us at: Nomatterwhatdream@gmail.com

Like us on Facebook and follow us on Twitter

Facebook: facebook.com/NoMatterWhatDream

Twitter: @Dream_RMitchell